MW01491170

ARRL's
General Q&A

WITHDRAWN

Cover photo: ————————————

Rhonda Leonard, KC1KYN, and Alex Norstrom,
KC1RMO, operate out of W1HQ in Newington, CT.

The National Association for
Amateur Radio®
225 Main Street, Newington, CT 06111-1400
www.arrl.org

Copyright © 2023 by The American
Radio Relay League, Inc.

Copyright secured under the Pan-American
Convention

International copyright secured.

All rights reserved. No part of this work may
be reproduced in any form except by written
permission of the publisher. All rights of
translation are reserved.

Printed in the USA

Quedan reservados todos los derechos

ISBN: 978-1-62595-172-4

Seventh Edition

This book may be used for General license exams given beginning July 1, 2023. The ARRL website (**arrl.org**) will have news about any rules changes affecting the General class license or any of the material in this book.

Feedback: We're interested in hearing your comments on this book and what you'd like to see in future editions. Please email comments to us at **pubsfdbk@arrl.org**, including your name, call sign, email address, and the title, edition, and printing of this book.

We strive to produce books without errors. Sometimes mistakes do occur, however. When we become aware of problems in our books (other than obvious typographical errors), we post corrections on the ARRL website. If you think you have found an error, please check **arrl.org** for corrections and supplemental material. If you don't find a correction there, please let us know by sending email to **pubsfdbk@arrl.org**.

Contents

General Class (Element 3) Syllabus

Effective July 1, 2023 to June 30, 2027
SUBELEMENT G1 — COMMISSION'S RULES
[5 Exam Questions — 5 Groups] 57 Questions

SUBELEMENT G2 — OPERATING PROCEDURES
[5 Exam Questions — 5 Groups] 60 Questions

SUBELEMENT G7 — PRACTICAL CIRCUITS
[3 Exam Questions — 3 Groups] 38 Questions

115 G7A — Power supplies; schematic symbols
122 G7B — Digital circuits; amplifiers and oscillators
127 G7C— Transceiver design; filters; oscillators; digital signal processing (DSP)

SUBELEMENT G8 — SIGNALS AND EMISSIONS
[3 Exam Questions — 3 Groups] 43 Questions

135 G8A — Carriers and modulation: AM, FM, and single sideband; modulation envelope; digital modulation; overmodulation; link budgets and link margins
142 G8B — Frequency changing; bandwidths of various modes; deviation; intermodulation
147 G8C — Digital emission modes

SUBELEMENT G9 — ANTENNAS AND FEED LINES
[4 Exam Questions — 4 Groups] 46 Questions

152 G9A — Feed lines: characteristic impedance and attenuation; standing wave ratio (SWR) calculation, measurement, and effects; antenna feed point matching
157 G9B — Basic dipole and monopole antennas
162 G9C — Directional antennas
167 G9D — Specialized antenna types and applications

SUBELEMENT G0 — ELECTRICAL AND RF SAFETY
[2 Exam Questions — 2 Groups] 25 Questions

171 G0A — RF safety principles, rules and guidelines; routine station evaluation
178 G0B — Station safety: electrical shock, grounding, fusing, interlocks, and wiring; antenna and tower safety

When to Expect New Books

A Question Pool Committee (QPC) consisting of representatives from the various Volunteer Examiner Coordinators (VECs) prepares the license question pools. The QPC establishes a schedule for revising and implementing new Question Pools. The current Question Pool revision schedule is as follows:

Question Pool	Current Study Guides	Valid Through
Technician (Element 2)	*The ARRL Ham Radio License Manual*, 5th Edition *ARRL's Tech Q&A*, 8th Edition	June 30, 2026
General (Element 3)	*The ARRL General Class License Manual*, 10th edition *ARRL's General Q&A*, 7th Edition	June 30, 2027
Amateur Extra (Element 4)	*The ARRL Extra Class License Manual*, 12th Edition *ARRL's Extra Q&A*, 5th Edition	June 30, 2024

As new question pools are released, ARRL will produce new study materials before their effective dates. As the new question pool schedules are confirmed, the information will be published on the ARRL website at **arrl.org**.

How to Use
This Book

To earn a General class Amateur Radio license, you must pass (or receive credit for) FCC Elements 2 (Technician class) and 3 (General class). This book is designed to help you prepare for and pass the Element 3 exam. If you do not already have a Technician class license, you will need study materials for the Element 2 (Technician) exam.

The Element 3 exam consists of 35 questions about Amateur Radio rules, theory and practice, as well as some basic electronics. A passing grade is 74%, so you must answer 26 of the 35 questions correctly.

ARRL's General Q&A follows subelements G1 through G0 in the General class syllabus. The questions and multiple choice answers in this book are printed exactly as they appear on the exam. (Be careful: the position of the answers may be scrambled so you can't simply memorize an answer letter for each question.) In this book, the letter of the correct answer is printed in **boldface** type just before the explanation.

The ARRL also maintains a special web page for General class students at **arrl.org/general-class-license-manual**. Be sure to visit that web page during your preparation for the exam.

What We Assume About You

You don't have to be a technical guru or an expert operator to upgrade to General class! As you progress through the material, you'll build on the basic science of radio and electricity you mastered for Technician. No advanced mathematics is required and tutorials are listed at **arrl.org/general-class-license-manual**. As with the Technician license, mastering rules and regulations will require learning some new words and a few numbers. You should have a basic calculator, which you'll also be allowed to use during the license exam.

ARRL's General Q&A can be used either by an individual student, studying on his or her own, or as part of a licensing class taught by an instructor. Either way, you'll find that having a friend to study with makes learning the material more fun.

Don't hesitate to ask for help! If you can't find the answer in the book or at the website, email your question to the ARRL's New Ham Desk, **newham@arrl.org**. The ARRL's experts will answer directly or connect you with another ham that can answer your questions.

Process

When you're ready, you'll need to find a test session. If you're in a licensing class, the instructor will help you find and register for a session. Otherwise, you can find a test session by using the ARRL's web page for finding exams, **arrl.org/exam**. If you can register for the test session in advance, do so. Other sessions, such as those at hamfests or conventions, are available to anyone that shows up or walk-ins. You may have to wait for an available space though, so go early!

As for all amateur exams, the General class exam is administered by Volunteer Examiners (VEs). All VEs are certified by a Volunteer Examiner Coordinator (VEC) such as the ARRL VEC. A VEC trains and certifies VEs and processes the FCC paperwork for their test sessions.

Bring your original current license or Certificate of Successful Completion of Examination (CSCE) and a photocopy (to send with the application). You'll need two forms of identification including at least one photo ID, such as a driver's license, passport or employer's identity card. Know your Social Security Number (SSN). You can bring pencils or pens, blank scratch paper and a calculator, but any kind of computer or on-line device is prohibited. You can also take your exam online. For a list of online VE teams, visit **arrl.org/online-exam-session**. for most online exam sessions you will need to know your FRN, which you can get directly from the FCC at **fcc.gov/wireless/systems-utilities/universal-licensing-system**.

The FCC allows Volunteer Examiners to use a range of procedures to accommodate applicants with various disabilities. If this applies to you, you'll still have to pass the test, but special exam procedures are available. Contact your local VE team or the Volunteer Examiner Coordinator (VEC) responsible for the test session you'll be attending. Or contact the ARRL/VEC Office at 225 Main St, Newington CT 06111-1494 or by phone at 860-594-0200.

Once you're signed in, you'll need to fill out a copy of the National Conference of Volunteer Examiner Coordinator's (NCVEC) Quick Form 605. This is an application for a new or upgraded license. It is used only at test sessions and for a VEC to process a license renewal or a license change. Do not use an NCVEC Quick Form 605 for any kind of application directly to the FCC — it will be rejected. After filling out the form, pay the current test fee and get ready. Good luck!

The Exam

The General test takes from 30 minutes to an hour. You will be given a question booklet and an answer sheet. Be sure to read the instructions, fill in all the necessary information and sign your name wherever it's required. Check to be sure your booklet has all the questions and be sure to mark the answer in the correct space for each question.

You don't have to answer the questions in order — skip the hard ones and go back to them. If you read the answers carefully, you'll probably find that you can eliminate one or more "distracters." Of the remaining answers, only one will be the best. If you can't decide which is the correct answer, go ahead and guess. There is no penalty for an incorrect guess. When you're done, go back and check your

NCVEC QUICK-FORM 605 APPLICATION
AMATEUR OPERATOR/PRIMARY STATION LICENSE

SECTION 1 - TO BE COMPLETED BY APPLICANT
PLEASE PRINT LEGIBLY!

PRINT LAST NAME	SUFFIX (Jr., Sr.)	FIRST NAME	M.I.	AMATEUR RADIO CALL SIGN (IF LICENSED)

MAILING ADDRESS (Number and Street or P.O. Box)	FCC REGISTRATION NUMBER (FRN) (MANDATORY)
225 Main St	0009876543

CITY	STATE CODE	ZIP CODE	DAYTIME TELEPHONE NUMBER (Including Area Code)
Newington		06111	860-594-0200

EMAIL ADDRESS (MANDATORY)
KB1KJC@arrl.org

Basic Qualification Question -- *Answer Required in Order to Process Your Application*

Has the Applicant or any party to this application, or any party directly or indirectly controlling the Applicant, ever been convicted

of a felony by any state or federal court? ☐ YES ☐ NO

If "YES", see "FCC BASIC QUALIFICATION QUESTION INSTRUCTIONS AND PROCEDURES" on the back of this form.

I HEREBY APPLY FOR [Make an X in the appropriate box(es)]:

☐ **EXAMINATION** for a new license grant

☐ **EXAMINATION** for **upgrade** of my license class

☐ **CHANGE** my **name** on my license to my new name

Former Name: _____
　　　　　　(Last name) (Suffix)　(First name)　(MI)

☐ **CHANGE** my mailing address to **above** address

☐ **CHANGE** my station **call sign** systematically

Applicant's Initials To Confirm _____

☐ **RENEWAL** of my license grant

Exp. Date: _____

I certify that:
- I waive any claim to the use of any particular frequency regardless of prior use by license or otherwise;
- All statements and attachments are true, complete, and correct to the best of my knowledge and belief and are made in good faith;
- I am not a representative of a foreign government;
- I am not subject to a denial of Federal benefits pursuant to Section 5301of the Anti-Drug Abuse Act of 1988, 21 U.S.C. § 862;
- The construction of my station will NOT be an action which is likely to have a significant environmental effect [See 47 CFR Sections 1.1301-1.1319 and Section 97.13(a)];
- I have read and WILL COMPLY with Section 97.13(c) of the Commission's Rules regarding RADIO FREQUENCY (RF) RADIATION SAFETY and the amateur service section of OST/OET Bulletin Number 65.

Signature of Applicant:

X *Maria Semma*　　　　Date Signed: _____

SECTION 2 - TO BE COMPLETED BY ALL ADMINISTERING VEs

Applicant is qualified for operator license class:

☐ NO NEW LICENSE OR UPGRADE WAS EARNED

☐ TECHNICIAN　　Element 2

☐ GENERAL　　Elements 2 and 3

☐ AMATEUR EXTRA　　Elements 2, 3, and 4

DATE OF EXAMINATION SESSION
EXAMINATION SESSION LOCATION
VEC ORGANIZATION
ARRL VEC
VEC RECEIPT DATE

I CERTIFY THAT I HAVE COMPLIED WITH THE ADMINISTERING VE REQUIREMENTS IN PART 97 OF THE COMMISSION'S RULES AND WITH THE INSTRUCTIONS PROVIDED BY THE COORDINATING VEC AND THE FCC.

1st VE's NAME (Print First, MI, Last, Suffix)	VE's STATION CALL SIGN	VE's SIGNATURE (Must match name)	DATE SIGNED
		Bunny Xates	
2nd VE's NAME (Print First, MI, Last, Suffix)	VE's STATION CALL SIGN	VE's SIGNATURE (Must match name)	DATE SIGNED
		Rose-ann Lawrence	
3rd VE's NAME (Print First, MI, Last, Suffix)	VE's STATION CALL SIGN	VE's SIGNATURE (Must match name)	DATE SIGNED
		Flory Green	

DO NOT SEND THIS FORM TO FCC -- THIS IS NOT AN FCC FORM.
IF THIS FORM IS SENT TO FCC, FCC WILL RETURN IT TO YOU WITHOUT ACTION.

NCVEC FORM 605 - July 2022
FOR VE/VEC USE ONLY - Page 1

This sample NCVEC Quick Form 605 shows how your form will look after you have completed your upgrade to General.

answers and double-check your arithmetic — there's no rush!

Once you've answered all 35 questions, the Volunteer Examiners will grade and verify your test results. Assuming you've passed (congratulations!) you'll fill out a Certificate of Successful Completion of Examination. The exam organizers will submit your results to the FCC while you keep the CSCE as evidence that you've passed your General test.

If you are licensed and already have a call sign, you can begin using your new privileges immediately. When you give your call sign, append "/AG" (on CW or digital modes) or "temporary AG" (on phone). As soon as your name and call sign appear in the FCC's database of licensees, typically a week to 10 days later, you can stop adding the suffix. The CSCE is good for 365 days in case there's a delay or problem with license processing or you decide to upgrade to Extra class right away.

If you don't pass, don't be discouraged! You might be able to take another version of the test right then and there if the session organizers can accommodate you. Even if you decide to try again later, you now know just how the test session feels — you'll be more relaxed and ready next time. The ham bands are full of hams who took their General test more than once before passing. You'll be in good company!

FCC and ARRL/VEC Licensing Resources

After you pass your exam, the examiners will file all of the necessary paperwork so that your license will be granted by the Federal Communications Commission (FCC). In a few days, you will see your new call sign in the FCC's database via the ARRL's website.

When you passed your Technician exam, you may have applied for your FCC Federal Registration Number (FRN). This allows you to access the information for any FCC licenses you may have and to request modifications to them. These functions are available via the FCC's Universal Licensing System website (**fcc.gov/wireless/systems-utilities/universal-licensing-system**) and complete instructions for using the site are available at **arrl.org/universal-licensing-system**.

The ARRL/VEC can also process license renewals and modifications for you as described at **arrl.org/call-sign-renewals-or-changes**.

Books to Help
You Learn

As you study the material on the licensing exam, you will have lots of other questions about the how and why of Amateur Radio. The following references, available from your local bookstore or the ARRL (**www.arrl.org/shop**) will help "fill in the blanks" and give you a broader picture of the hobby:

• *ARRL Operating Manual.* With in-depth sections on the most popular ham radio activities, this is your guide to digital mode operating, radiosport, award programs, DXing and more.

• *Understanding Basic Electronics* by Walter Banzhaf, WB1ANE. Students who want more technical background about electronics should take a look at this book. It covers the fundamentals of electricity and electronics that are the foundation of all radio.

• *Basic Radio* by Joel Hallas, W1ZR. Students who want more technical background about radio theory should take a look at this book. It covers the key building blocks of receivers, transmitters, antennas, and propagation.

• *ARRL Handbook.* This is the grandfather of all Amateur Radio references and belongs on the shelf of hams. Almost any topic you can think of in Amateur Radio technology is represented here.

• *ARRL Antenna Book.* After the radio itself, all radio depends on antennas. This book provides information on every common type of amateur antenna, feed lines and related topics, and practical construction tips and techniques.

Online Practice Exams

While you're studying and when you feel like you're ready for the actual exam you can get some good practice by taking an online amateur radio exams. The exams are free and you can take them over and over again in complete privacy. To get started, visit the ARRL Exam Review for Ham Radio web page at **arrl.org/examreview**.

These exams are quite realistic and you get quick feedback about the questions you didn't answer correctly. When you find yourself passing the practice exams by a comfortable margin, you'll be ready for the real thing!

About ARRL

We're the American Radio Relay League, Inc. — better known as ARRL. We're the largest membership association for the amateur radio hobby and service in the US. For over 100 years, we have been the primary source of information about amateur radio, offering a variety of benefits and services to our members, as well as the larger amateur radio community. We publish books on amateur radio, as well as four magazines covering a variety of radio communication interests. In addition, we provide technical advice and assistance to amateur radio enthusiasts, support several education programs, and sponsor a variety of operating events.

One of the primary benefits we offer to the ham radio community is in representing the interests of amateur radio operators before federal regulatory bodies advocating for meaningful access to the radio spectrum. ARRL also serves as the international secretariat of the International Amateur Radio Union, which performs a similar role internationally, advocating for amateur radio interests before the International Telecommunication Union and the World Radiocommunication Conference.

Today, we proudly serve nearly 160,000 members, both in the US and internationally, through our national headquarters and flagship amateur radio station, W1AW, in Newington, Connecticut. Every year we welcome thousands of new licensees to our membership, and we hope you will join us. Let us be a part of your amateur radio journey. Visit www.arrl.org/join for more information.

225 Main Street
Newington, CT 06111-1400 USA
Tel: 860-594-0200
FAX: 860-594-0259
Email: membership@arrl.org
arrl.org

Get more from your General Class License with ARRL Membership

Membership in ARRL offers unique opportunities to advance and share your knowledge of amateur radio. For over 100 years, advancing the art, science, and enjoyment of amateur radio has been our mission. Your membership helps to ensure that new generations of hams continue to reap the benefits of the amateur radio community.

Here are just a few of the benefits you will receive with your annual membership. For a complete list visit, arrl.org/membership.

KNOWLEDGE

ARRL offers you a wealth of knowledge to advance your skills with lifelong learning courses, local clubs where you can meet and share ideas, and publications to help you keep up with the latest information from the world of ham radio.

ADVOCACY

ARRL is a strong national voice for preserving and protecting access to Amateur Radio Service frequencies.

SERVICES

From free FCC license renewals, to our Technical Information Service that answers calls and emails about your operating and technical concerns, ARRL offers a range of member services.

RESOURCES

Digital resources including email forwarding, product review archives, e-newsletters, and more.

PUBLICATIONS

Members receive digital access to all four ARRL monthly and bimonthly publications – *QST*, the membership journal of ARRL; *On the Air*, an introduction to the world of amateur radio; *QEX*, which covers topics related to amateur radio and radio communications experimentation, and *National Contest Journal* (*NCJ*), covering radio contesting.

Two Easy Ways to Join

CALL
Member Services toll free at **1-888-277-5289**

ONLINE
Go to our secure website at **arrl.org/join**

ARRL Membership Application

☐ **New**   ☐ **Renew**   ☐ **Previous Member**   ☐ **Unlicensed**

Name_____ Call Sign _____

Address _____

City _____State _____ ZIP _____

Email _____ Phone_____

Date of Birth _____/_____/_____

My Family Member is Joining or Renewing: ($10 per member)

Name_____ Call Sign _____

Name_____ Call Sign _____

☐ I do not want my name and address made available for non-ARRL related mailings

Your Annual Membership Dues –
Circle Your Choice

	3 Years	2 Years	1 Year
Diamond Club (includes 1-year ARRL Membership)			$95
Diamond Club for current Life Members			$50
Standard Membership	$140	$95	$49
International (Digital Only)	$140	$95	$49
International (with mailed QST)	$217	$147	$76
Blind	$30	$20	$10
Family	$30	$20	$10
Student			$25

Add on ARRL Subscriptions Annual rate – 6 issues

	U.S.	U.S. 1st Class	International
QEX	$29	$40	$35
NCJ	$25	$34	$32
OTA	$40		

Choose your print magazine –
Check One

____ **QST** (12 monthly issues)

____ **On the Air** (6 bimonthly issues) US Only

____ **Digital Only**, no print magazine

Diamond Club $_____

(minimum $95 per year; includes 1-year of ARRL Membership and tax deductible contribution)

$_____ TOTAL

Dues are subject to change without notice and are non-refundable.

Toll Free (US) 1-888-277-5289 or 860-594-0200 • ARRL, 225 Main St., Newington, CT 06111-1400
membership@arrl.org • arrl.org/join

Commission's Rules

[5 Exam Questions — 5 Groups]

G1A — General class control operator frequency privileges; primary and secondary allocations

G1A01   On which HF and/or MF amateur bands are there portions where General class licensees cannot transmit?

A. 60 meters, 20 meters, 17 meters, and 12 meters
B. 160 meters,60 meters, 15 meters, and 12 meters
C. 80 meters, 40 meters, 20 meters, and 15 meters
D. 80 meters, 20 meters, 15 meters, and 10 meters

(C)   These are the bands on which the entire range of mode-restricted segments (such as phone or CW/data) are open to all license classes that have access to the band. General, Advanced, and Extra class licensees all have access to the entire band. [97.301(d)] [*General Class License Manual*, page 3-8]

G1A02   On which of the following bands is phone operation prohibited?

A. 160 meters
B. 30 meters
C. 17 meters
D. 12 meters

(B)   The 30 meter band is restricted to CW, RTTY, and data transmissions only. Image transmission is also prohibited on the 60 meter band. [97.305] [*General Class License Manual*, page 3-8]

G1A03   On which of the following bands is image transmission prohibited?

A. 160 meters
B. 30 meters
C. 20 meters
D. 12 meters

(B)   See G1A02. [97.305] [*General Class License Manual*, page 3-8]

G1A04 Which of the following amateur bands is restricted to communication only on specific channels, rather than frequency ranges?

A. 11 meters
B. 12 meters
C. 30 meters
D. 60 meters

(D) In the US, Amateur Radio is a secondary service to government stations on 60 meters. By limiting amateur operation to specific channels, it is easier for hams to tell when government stations are present and to avoid interfering with them. [97.303 (h)] [*General Class License Manual*, page 3-8]

G1A05 On which of the following frequencies are General class licensees prohibited from operating as control operator?

A. 7.125 MHz to 7.175 MHz
B. 28.000 MHz to 28.025 MHz
C. 21.275 MHz to 21.300 MHz
D. All of the above

(A) General class licensees have access to the following portions of the 40 meter band (f = 300 / 40 = 7.5 MHz): 7.025 – 7.125 MHz on CW/RTTY/Data and from 7.175 – 7.300 MHz on CW/Phone/Image. [97.301(d)] [*General Class License Manual*, page 3-8]

US Amateur Bands

US AMATEUR POWER LIMITS — FCC 97.313 An amateur station must use the minimum transmitter power necessary to carry out the desired communications. (b) No station may transmit with a transmitter power exceeding 1.5 kW PEP.

Amateurs wishing to operate on either 2,200 or 630 meters must first register with the Utilities Technology Council online at **https://utc.org/plc-database-amateur-notification-process/** You need only register once for each band.

2,200 Meters (135 kHz)

E,A,G

135.7 kHz   1 W EIRP maximum   137.8 kHz

630 Meters (472 kHz)

E,A,G

472 kHz   479 kHz
5 W EIRP maximum, except in Alaska within 496 miles of Russia where the power limit is 1 W EIRP.

160 Meters (1.8 MHz)
Avoid interference to radiolocation operations from 1.900 to 2.000 MHz

E,A,G

1.800   1.900   2.000 MHz

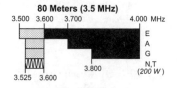

80 Meters (3.5 MHz)

3.500 3.600 3.700   4.000 MHz

E
A
G
N,T
(200 W)

3.525 3.600   3.800

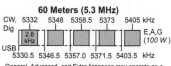

60 Meters (5.3 MHz)

CW, Dig   5332   5348   5358.5   5373   5405 kHz

2.8 kHz

E,A,G
(100 W)

USB
5330.5 5346.5 5357.0 5371.5 5403.5 kHz

General, Advanced, and Extra licensees may operate on a secondary basis with a maximum ERP of 100 W (relative to a half-wave dipole antenna).

40 Meters (7 MHz)

7.000 7.075 7.100   7.300 MHz

ITU 1,3 and FCC region 2 west of 130° west or below 20° north

Region 2 only

7.175
N,T *outside region 2*

E
A
G
N,T
(200 W)

7.025   7.125

See Sections 97.305(c), 97.307(f)(11) and 97.301(e). These exemptions do not apply to stations in the continental US.

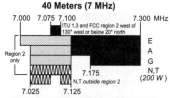

30 Meters (10.1 MHz)
Avoid interference to fixed services outside the US.

200 Watts PEP   E,A,G

10.100   10.150 MHz

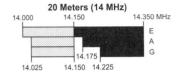

20 Meters (14 MHz)

14.000 14.150 14.350 MHz

E
A
G

14.175

14.025 14.150 14.225

17 Meters (18 MHz)

E,A,G

18.068 18.110 18.168 MHz

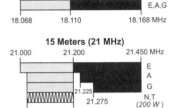

15 Meters (21 MHz)

21.000 21.200 21.450 MHz

E
A
G

21.225
21.275

N,T
(*200 W*)

21.025 21.200

12 Meters (24 MHz)

E,A,G

24.890 24.930 24.990 MHz

10 Meters (28 MHz)

28.000 28.300 29.700 MHz

E,A,G
N,T
(*200 W*)

28.000 28.500

6 Meters (50 MHz)

50.1

E,A,G,T

50.0 54.0 MHz

2 Meters (144 MHz)

144.1

E,A,G,T

144.0 148.0 MHz

1.25 Meters (222 MHz)

E,A,G,T
N (*25 W*)

219.0 220.0
222.0 225.0 MHz

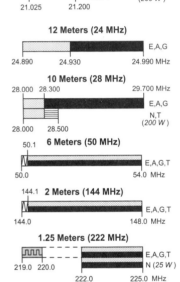

ARRL
We're At Your Service

ARRL Headquarters:
860-594-0200 (Fax 860-594-0259)
email: hq@arrl.org

Publication Orders:
www.arrl.org/shop
Toll-Free 1-888-277-5289 (860-594-0355)
email: orders@arrl.org

Membership/Circulation Desk:
www.arrl.org/membership
Toll-Free 1-888-277-5289 (860-594-0338)
email: membership@arrl.org

Getting Started in Amateur Radio:
Toll-Free 1-800-326-3942 (860-594-0355)
email: newham@arrl.org

Exams: 860-594-0300 email: vec@arrl.org

KEY

Note:
CW operation is permitted throughout all amateur bands.

MCW is authorized above 50.1 MHz, except for 144.0-144.1 and 219-220 MHz.

Test transmissions are authorized above 51 MHz, except for 219-220 MHz

= RTTY and data
= phone and image
= CW *only*
= SSB phone
= USB phone, CW, RTTY, and data.
= Fixed digital message forwarding systems *only*

E = Amateur Extra
A = Advanced
G = General
T = Technician
N = Novice

See *www.arrl.org/band-plan* for detailed band plans.

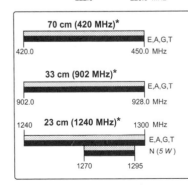

70 cm (420 MHz)*

E,A,G,T

420.0 450.0 MHz

33 cm (902 MHz)*

E,A,G,T

902.0 928.0 MHz

23 cm (1240 MHz)*

1240 1300 MHz

E,A,G,T
N (*5 W*)

1270 1295

*Geographical and power restrictions may apply to all bands above 420 MHz. See FCC Part 97.303 for information about your area.

All licensees except Novices are authorized all modes on the following frequencies:

2300-2310 MHz	47.0-47.2 GHz
2390-2450 MHz	76.0-81.0 GHz
3400-3450 MHz	122.25-123.0 GHz
5650-5925 MHz	134-141 GHz
10.0-10.5 GHz ‡	241-250 GHz
24.0-24.25 GHz	All above 275 GHz

‡ No pulse emissions

Copyright © ARRL 2023 **rev. 2/10/2023**

G1A06 **Which of the following applies when the FCC rules designate the amateur service as a secondary user on a band?**

A. Amateur stations must record the call sign of the primary service station before operating on a frequency assigned to that station
B. Amateur stations may use the band only during emergencies
C. Amateur stations must not cause harmful interference to primary users and must accept interference from primary users
D. Amateur stations may only operate during specific hours of the day, while primary users are permitted 24-hour use of the band

(C) In some bands, amateur share access with other services. These are *secondary amateur allocations*, meaning that stations in the primary services have priority. Amateur stations in secondary or shared allocations must not cause harmful interference to stations in the primary service. If you are operating in a secondary amateur allocation and a station in the primary service begins transmitting, you must move to a clear frequency or stop transmitting. [97.303] *[General Class License Manual*, page 3-7]

G1A07 **On which amateur frequencies in the 10-meter band may stations with a General class control operator transmit CW emissions?**

A. 28.000 MHz to 28.025 MHz only
B. 28.000 MHz to 28.300 MHz only
C. 28.025 MHz to 28.300 MHz only
D. The entire band

(D) CW operation is permitted throughout all amateur bands. See the band plan on page two. [97.305(a)] *[General Class License Manual*, page 3-8]

G1A08 **Which HF bands have segments exclusively allocated to Amateur Extra licensees?**

A. All HF bands
B. 80 meters, 40 meters, 20 meters, and 15 meters
C. All HF bands except 160 meters and 10 meters
D. 60 meters, 30 meters, 17 meters, and 12 meters

(B) See the band plan on page two. [97.301(b)] *[General Class License Manual*, page 3-8]

G1A09 **Which of the following frequencies is within the General class portion of the 15-meter band?**
A. 14250 kHz
B. 18155 kHz
C. 21300 kHz
D. 24900 kHz

(C) General class licensees have access to the following portions of the 15 meter band (f = 300 / 15 = 20 MHz): 21.025 – 21.200 MHz on CW/RTTY/ Data and from 21.275 – 21.450 MHz on CW/Phone/Image. [97.301(d)] [*General Class License Manual*, page 3-8]

G1A10 **What portion of the 10-meter band is available for repeater use?**
A. The entire band
B. The portion between 28.1 MHz and 28.2 MHz
C. The portion between 28.3 MHz and 28.5 MHz
D. The portion above 29.5 MHz

(D) Repeater operation on HF is limited to the 10-meter band from 29.6 to 29.7 MHz. [97.205(b)] [*General Class License Manual*, page 3-8]

G1A11 **When General class licensees are not permitted to use the entire voice portion of a band, which portion of the voice segment is available to them?**
A. The lower frequency portion
B. The upper frequency portion
C. The lower frequency portion on frequencies below 7.3 MHz, and the upper portion on frequencies above 14.150 MHz
D. The upper frequency portion on frequencies below 7.3 MHz, and the lower portion on frequencies above 14.150 MHz

(B) If you look at the US Amateur Band chart available in the *General Class License Manual* or on the ARRL website at **www.arrl.org/graphical-frequency-allocations** you will see that in the bands on which there are mode-restricted segments, such as 80 meters, General class licensees have access to the higher frequencies of the segment. [97.301] [*General Class License Manual*, page 3-8]

G1B — Antenna structure limitations; good engineering and good amateur practice; beacon operation; prohibited transmissions; retransmitting radio signals

G1B01 What is the maximum height above ground for an antenna structure not near a public use airport without requiring notification to the FAA and registration with the FCC?

A. 50 feet
B. 100 feet
C. 200 feet
D. 250 feet

(C) FCC regulations require approval if your antenna would be more than 200 feet above ground level. This includes the antenna, the supports and anything else attached to the structure. (Additional FCC restrictions apply if the antenna is within about 4 miles of a public use airport or heliport.) [97.15(a)] [*General Class License Manual*, page 3-3]

G1B02 With which of the following conditions must beacon stations comply?

A. No more than one beacon station may transmit in the same band from the same station location
B. The frequency must be coordinated with the National Beacon Organization
C. The frequency must be posted on the internet or published in a national periodical
D. All these choices are correct

(A) A beacon station normally transmits a signal for operators to observe propagation and reception characteristics. For this purpose, FCC rules specifically allow an amateur beacon to transmit one-way communications. [97.203(b)] [*General Class License Manual*, page 3-8]

G1B03 Which of the following is a purpose of a beacon station as identified in the FCC rules?

A. Observation of propagation and reception
B. Automatic identification of repeaters
C. Transmission of bulletins of general interest to amateur radio licensees
D. All these choices are corect

(A) See G1B02. [97.3(a)(9)] [*General Class License Manual*, page 3-8]

G1B04 **Which of the following transmissions is permitted for all amateur stations?**

A. Unidentified transmissions of less than 10 seconds duration for test purposes only
B. Automatic retransmission of other amateur signals by any amateur station
C. Occasional retransmission of weather and propagation forecast information from US government stations
D. Encrypted messages, if not intended to facilitate a criminal act

(C) In general, you can't retransmit a broadcast but there are exceptions. Broadcasts of weather or propagation predictions from a US government station may be retransmitted, as long as you only do it occasionally. [97.113(c)] [*General Class License Manual*, page 3-14]

G1B05 **Which of the following one-way transmissions are permitted?**

A. Unidentified test transmissions of less than 10 seconds in duration
B. Transmissions to assist with learning the International Morse code
C. Regular transmissions offering equipment for sale, if intended for amateur radio use
D. All these choices are correct

(B) Generally, one-way transmissions are not permitted but there is an exception for "code practice." [97.111((5)(b)] [*General Class License Manual*, page 3-14]

G1B06 **Under what conditions are state and local governments permitted to regulate amateur radio antenna structures?**

A. Under no circumstances, FCC rules take priority
B. At any time and to any extent necessary to accomplish a legitimate purpose of the state or local entity, provided that proper filings are made with the FCC
C. Only when such structures exceed 50 feet in height and are clearly visible 1,000 feet from the structure
D. Amateur Service communications must be reasonably accommodated, and regulations must constitute the minimum practical to accommodate a legitimate purpose of the state or local entity

(D) Local building rules and codes may also affect your ability to put up towers and antennas. In the FCC rule known as PRB-1, the FCC requires that Amateur Service communications must be reasonably accommodated. Any regulations must be the minimum practical and have a legitimate purpose. [97.15(b), PRB-1, 101 FCC 2d 952 (1985)] [*General Class License Manual*, page 3-1]

G1B07 **What are the restrictions on the use of abbreviations or procedural signals in the amateur service?**

A. Only "Q" signals are permitted
B. They may be used if they do not obscure the meaning of a message
C. They are not permitted
D. They are limited to those expressly listed in Part 97 of the FCC rules

(B) The use of common abbreviations and procedural signals is standard practice and does not obscure the meaning of a message because their meaning is well known. Any use of abbreviations or codes for the purpose of obscuring the meaning of a communication is prohibited. [97.113(a)(4)] [*General Class License Manual*, page 3-14]

G1B08 **When is it permissible to communicate with amateur stations in countries outside the areas administered by the Federal Communications Commission?**

A. Only when the foreign country has a formal third-party agreement filed with the FCC
B. When the contact is with amateurs in any country except those whose administrations have notified the ITU that they object to such communications
C. Only when the contact is with amateurs licensed by a country which is a member of the United Nations, or by a territory possessed by such a country
D. Only when the contact is with amateurs licensed by a country which is a member of the International Amateur Radio Union, or by a territory possessed by such a country

(B) It is also permitted for US amateurs to communicate with amateur stations in countries outside the areas administered by the Federal Communications Commission *unless* the country's administration has notified the ITU that it objects to such communications. [97.111(a)(1)] [*General Class License Manual*, page 3-14]

G1B09 **On what HF frequencies are automatically controlled beacons permitted?**

A. On any frequency if power is less than 1 watt
B. On any frequency if transmissions are in Morse code
C. 21.08 MHz to 21.09 MHz
D. 28.20 MHz to 28.30 MHz

(D) 28.2 to 28.3 MHz is the only HF band segment where automatically controlled beacon operation is authorized by the FCC rules. [97.203(d)] [*General Class License Manual*, page 3-8]

G1B10 **What is the power limit for beacon stations?**

A. 10 watts PEP output
B. 20 watts PEP output
C. 100 watts PEP output
D. 200 watts PEP output

(C)   100 watts of output power is a good compromise, enabling a beacon station to transmit a signal strong enough to be heard when propagation isn't the best. Similarly, when propagation is good, a 100-watt signal is not so strong as to cause interference to stations on nearby frequencies. [97.203(c)] [*General Class License Manual*, page 3-8]

G1B11 **Who or what determines "good engineering and good amateur practice," as applied to the operation of an amateur station in all respects not covered by the Part 97 rules?**

A. The FCC
B. The control operator
C. The IEEE
D. The ITU

(A)   The FCC does not publish a list of what constitutes "good engineering and good amateur practice" because the state of the radio art is continually improving. Nevertheless, when questions arise, the FCC is the agency that determines what standards should be applied. [97.101(a)] [*General Class License Manual*, page 3-15]

G1C — Transmitter power regulations; data emission standards; 60-meter operation requirements

G1C01   What is the maximum transmitter power an amateur station may use on 10.140 MHz?

A. 200 watts PEP output
B. 1000 watts PEP output
C. 1500 watts PEP output
D. 2000 watts PEP output

(A)   The general rule is that maximum power is limited to 1500 watts PEP output, although there are exceptions where less power is allowed. One such exception is the 30 meter band, 10.100 – 10.150 MHz, where the maximum power output for US amateurs is 200 watts. [97.313(c)(1)] [*General Class License Manual*, page 3-15]

G1C02   What is the maximum transmitter power an amateur station may use on the 12-meter band?

A. 50 watts PEP output
B. 200 watts PEP output
C. 1500 watts PEP output
D. An effective radiated power equivalent to 100 watts from a half-wave dipole

(C)   The maximum power allowed is 1500 watts PEP output from 24.890 – 24.990 MHz. See also G1C01. [97.313(a),(b)] [*General Class License Manual*, page 3-15]

G1C03   What is the maximum bandwidth permitted by FCC rules for amateur radio stations transmitting on USB frequencies in the 60-meter band?

A. 2.8 kHz
B. 5.6 kHz
C. 1.8 kHz
D. 3 kHz

(A)   The FCC Rules for operating on the amateur 60 meter band tell us that "Amateur stations must ensure that their transmission occupies only the 2.8 kHz centered around each" of the operating channels. That means the maximum transmitted bandwidth of an upper sideband signal is 2.8 kHz. A properly adjusted SSB transmitter normally has a bandwidth of 2.5 to 2.8 kHz. This bandwidth limitation also applies to digital signals being transmitted on the 60 meter band. [97.303(h)(1)] [*General Class License Manual*, page 3-15]

G1C04 **Which of the following is required by the FCC rules when operating in the 60-meter band?**

A. If you are using an antenna other than a dipole, you must keep a record of the gain of your antenna
B. You must keep a record of the date, time, frequency, power level, and stations worked
C. You must keep a record of all third-party traffic
D. You must keep a record of the manufacturer of your equipment and the antenna used

(A) If you operate on 60 meters with any antenna other than a dipole, the FCC also requires you to keep a record of the antenna gain calculations or manufacturer's data. [97.303(i)]] [*General Class License Manual*, page 3-15]

G1C05 **What is the limit for transmitter power on the 28 MHz band for a General Class control operator?**

A. 100 watts PEP output
B. 1000 watts PEP output
C. 1500 watts PEP output
D. 2000 watts PEP output

(C) Novice and Technician licensees operating on HF are limited to 200 W PEP output. General, Advanced, and Extra licensees may use full 1500 W PEP output in the former Novice segments on 80, 40, and 15 meters. [97.313] [*General Class License Manual*, page 3-15]

G1C06 **What is the limit for transmitter power on the 1.8 MHz band?**

A. 200 watts PEP output
B. 1000 watts PEP output
C. 1200 watts PEP output
D. 1500 watts PEP output

(D) The maximum power allowed is 1500 watts PEP output on the entire band. See also G1C01. [97.313] [*General Class License Manual*, page 3-14]

G1C07 What must be done before using a new digital protocol on the air?

    A. Type-certify equipment to FCC standards
    B. Obtain an experimental license from the FCC
    C. Publicly document the technical characteristics of the protocol
    D. Submit a rule-making proposal to the FCC describing the codes and methods of the technique

(C) Amateurs are actively experimenting and innovating with digital modes. There are new protocols being introduced all the time. The FCC recognizes the need for amateurs to receive and understand signals must be balanced with the benefits of innovation. That is why the FCC requires the technical characteristics of the protocol be publicly documented before using it on the air. That can be as simple as posting the protocol's rules on a web page or in a magazine. [97.309(a)(4)] [*General Class License Manual*, page 3-16]

Withdrawn

G1C08 What is the maximum symbol rate permitted for RTTY or data emission transmitted at frequencies below 28 MHz?

    A. 56 kilobaud
    B. 19.6 kilobaud
    C. 1200 baud
    D. 300 baud

(D) The symbol rate of digital signals is restricted to make sure they do not consume too much bandwidth at the expense of other modes. Table G1.1 shows the limits by band. [97.307(f)(3)] [*General Class License Manual*, page 3-17]

G1C09 What is the maximum power limit on the 60-meter band?

    A. 1500 watts PEP
    B. 10 watts RMS
    C. ERP of 100 watts PEP with respect to a dipole
    D. ERP of 100 watts PEP with respect to an isotropic antenna

(C) Amateurs are restricted to 100 W ERP with respect to a half-wave dipole on the 60-meter band (5 MHz) with a maximum signal bandwidth of 2.8 kHz. [97.313(i)] [*General Class License Manual*, page 3-16]

Table G1.1

Maximum Symbol Rates and Bandwidth

Band	Symbol Rate (baud)	Bandwidth (kHz)
160 through 10 m	300	1
10 m	1200	1
6 m, 2 m	19.6k	20
1.25 m, 70 cm	56k	100
33 cm and above	no limit	entire band

withdrawn

G1C10 What is the maximum symbol rate permitted for RTTY or data emission transmissions on the 10-meter band?

A. 56 kilobaud
B. 19.6 kilobaud
C. 1200 baud
D. 300 baud

(C) See G1C08. [97.305(c), 97.307(f)(4)] [*General Class License Manual,* page 3-17]

G1C11 What measurement is specified by FCC rules that regulate maximum power?

A. RMS output from the transmitter
B. RMS input to the antenna
C. PEP input to the antenna
D. PEP output from the transmitter

(D) See G1C01. [97.313] [*General Class License Manual,* page 3-16]

G1D — Volunteer Examiners and Volunteer Examiner Coordinators; temporary identification; element credit; remote operation

G1D01 Who may receive partial credit for the elements represented by an expired Amateur Radio license?

A. Any person who can demonstrate that they once held an FCC-issued General, Advanced, or Amateur Extra class license that was not revoked by the FCC

B. Anyone who held an FCC-issued amateur radio license that expired not less than 5 and not more than 15 years ago

C. Any person who previously held an amateur license issued by another country, but only if that country has a current reciprocal licensing agreement with the FCC

D. Only persons who once held an FCC issued Novice, Technician, or Technician Plus license

(A) The rules grant "lifetime credit" for passing amateur exam elements 3 and 4. The applicant still has to pass element 2 (the Technician exam) however. [97.501, 97.505(a)] [*General Class License Manual*, page 3-3]

G1D02 What license examinations may you administer as an accredited Volunteer Examiner holding a General class operator license?

A. General and Technician

B. None, only Amateur Extra class licensees may be accredited

C. Technician only

D. Amateur Extra, General, and Technician

(C) Holders of a General class operator license may only administer examinations for the Technician class license. A General class licensee may participate as a VE in any exam session, but may not be the primary VE administering General or Extra class exams. [97.509(b)(3)(i)] [*General Class License Manual*, page 3-3]

G1D03 On which of the following band segments may you operate if you are a Technician class operator and have an unexpired Certificate of Successful Completion of Examination (CSCE) for General class privileges?

A Only the Technician band segments until your upgrade is posted in the FCC database

B. Only on the Technician band segments until you have a receipt for the FCC application fee payment

C. On any General or Technician class band segment

D. On any General or Technician class band segment except 30 meters and 60 meters

(C) You may begin using the General class privileges immediately on receiving your CSCE, but you must append the temporary identifier to your call sign as described in the discussion for G1D06. [97.9(b)] [*General Class License Manual*, page 3-4]

G1D04 Who must observe the administration of a Technician class license examination?

A. At least three Volunteer Examiners of General class or higher

B. At least two Volunteer Examiners of General class or higher

C. At least two Volunteer Examiners of Technician class or higher

D At least three Volunteer Examiners of Technician class

(A) All license exams are administered through the Volunteer Examiner Coordinator (VEC) system. VEs (Volunteer Examiners) must be accredited by a VEC. There must be three VEC-accredited VEs present at every exam session. Technician exams are administered by General class or higher VEs. [97.509(3)(i) (c)] [*General Class License Manual*, page 3-4]

G1D05 When operating a US station by remote control from outside the country, what license is required of the control operator?

A. A US operator/primary station license
B. Only an appropriate US operator/primary license and a special remote station permit from the FCC
C. Only a license from the foreign country, as long as the call sign includes identification of portable operation in the US
D. A license from the foreign country and a special remote station permit from the FCC

(A) The FCC is the agency in the United States charged with writing and administering the rules for US amateurs. FCC regulations apply to any amateur (US or foreign) who is operating where the FCC has jurisdiction. That includes all US states, possessions, and territories, as well as operation from US-flagged vessels operating in international waters, and remote operation of stations located within the US. [97.7] [*General Class License Manual*, page 3-4]

G1D06 Until an upgrade to General class is shown in the FCC database, when must a Technician licensee identify with "AG" after their call sign?

A. Whenever they operate using General class frequency privileges
B. Whenever they operate on any amateur frequency
C. Whenever they operate using Technician frequency privileges
D. A special identifier is not required if their General class license application has been filed with the FCC

(A) You must add a "temporary identifier" to your call sign so that stations receiving your transmissions can verify that you are authorized to transmit on that frequency. If a temporary identifier were not used between the time you pass your exam and the time at which your new privileges appear in the FCC database, it would appear that you were transmitting on a frequency for which you were not authorized. When you upgrade to Extra class, you'll append "temporary AE" to your call sign. [97.119(f)(2)] [*General Class License Manual*, page 3-4]

G1D07 **Volunteer Examiners are accredited by what organization?**

A. The Federal Communications Commission
B. The Universal Licensing System
C. A Volunteer Examiner Coordinator
D. The Wireless Telecommunications Bureau

(C) A Volunteer Examiner Coordinator (VEC) organization is responsible for certifying Volunteer Examiners and evaluating the results of all exam sessions administered by them. VECs also process all of the license application paperwork and submit it to the FCC. [97.509(b)(1)] [*General Class License Manual*, page 3-4]

G1D08 **Which of the following criteria must be met for a non-U.S. citizen to be an accredited Volunteer Examiner?**

A. The person must be a resident of the US for a minimum of 5 years
B. The person must hold an FCC granted amateur radio license of General class or above
C. The person's home citizenship must be in ITU region 2
D. None of these choices is correct; a non-US citizen cannot be a Volunteer Examiner

(B) A VE's citizenship does not matter, only whether the individual has demonstrated adequate knowledge of the US Amateur Service rules by passing the appropriate license exams. [97.509(b)(3)] [*General Class License Manual*, page 3-4]

G1D09 **How long is a Certificate of Successful Completion of Examination (CSCE) valid for exam element credit?**

A. 30 days
B. 180 days
C. 365 days
D. For as long as your current license is valid

(C) Although your new license class should appear in the FCC database within a few days of passing your examination, should there be a delay, remember that the CSCE is only good for 365 days. After that time, you'll have to re-take the examination! [97.9(b)] [*General Class License Manual*, page 3-4]

G1D10 What is the minimum age that one must be to qualify as an accredited Volunteer Examiner?

A. 16 years
B. 18 years
C. 21 years
D. There is no age limit

(B) 18 years old was determined to be an appropriate age to properly manage an amateur examination session. [97.509(b)(2)] [*General Class License Manual*, page 3-4]

G1D11 What action is required to obtain a new General class license after a previously held license has expired and the two-year grace period has passed?

A. They must have a letter from the FCC showing they once held an amateur or commercial license
B. There are no requirements other than being able to show a copy of the expired license
C. Contact the FCC to have the license reinstated
D. applicant must show proof of the appropriate expired license grant and pass the current Element 2 exam

(D) See G1D01. [97.505] [*General Class License Manual*, page 3-5]

G1D12 When operating a station in South America by remote control over the internet from the US, what regulations apply?

A. Those of both the remote station's country and the FCC
B. Those of the remote station's country and the FCC's third-party regulations
C. Only those of the remote station's country
D. Only those of the FCC

(C) Frequency sharing arrangements on the different bands are controlled by §97.303. Rule 97.307(f)(11) applies to US amateurs using phone in the Pacific and Caribbean. US amateurs operating abroad are required to abide by the appropriate regional frequency limits, subject to their host government's regulations. Similarly, US amateurs operating foreign stations remotely must abide by the rules of the remote station's country. [97.507] [*General Class License Manual*, page 3-1]

G1E — Control categories; repeater regulations; third-party rules; ITU regions; automatically controlled digital station

G1E01 Which of the following would disqualify a third party from participating in sending a message via an amateur station?

A. The third party's amateur license has been revoked and not reinstated
B. The third party is not a US citizen
C. The third party is speaking in a language other than English
D. All these choices are correct

(A) Third-party communication is available to anyone except someone with a revoked amateur license from any country. This prevents someone whose ability to make use of Amateur Radio was taken away from regaining access to amateur frequencies under the guise of third-party communications. [97.115(b)(2)] [*General Class License Manual*, page 3-12]

G1E02 When may a 10-meter repeater retransmit the 2-meter signal from a station that has a Technician class control operator?

A. Under no circumstances
B. Only if the station on 10-meters is operating under a Special Temporary Authorization allowing such retransmission
C. Only during an FCC-declared general state of communications emergency
D. Only if the 10-meter repeater control operator holds at least a General class license

(D) FCC rules allow any holder of an amateur license to be the control operator of a repeater. The control operator of the repeater must have privileges on the frequency on which the repeater is transmitting, however. A 10 meter repeater must have a General class or higher control operator because Technician and Novice licensees don't have privileges on the 10 meter repeater band. A 10 meter repeater may retransmit the 2 meter signal from a Technician class operator because the 10 meter control operator holds at least a General class license. [97.205(b)] [*General Class License Manual*, page 3-14]

G1E03 What is required to conduct communications with a digital station operating under automatic control outside the automatic control band segments?

A. The station initiating the contact must be under local or remote control
B. The interrogating transmission must be made by another automatically controlled station
C. No third-party traffic may be transmitted
D. The control operator of the interrogating station must hold an Amateur Extra Class license

(A) A human control operator must initiate and monitor communications with automatically controlled stations in order to prevent interference and insure proper operating practices. [97.221] [*General Class License Manual*, page 6-14]

G1E04 Which of the following conditions require a licensed amateur radio operator to take specific steps to avoid harmful interference to other users or facilities?

A. When operating within one mile of an FCC Monitoring Station
B. When using a band where the Amateur Service is secondary
C. When a station is transmitting spread spectrum emissions
D. All these choices are correct

(D) Aside from the general requirement to avoid causing harmful interference to other licensed stations and primary service licensees, there are several specific instances in which amateurs must take extra steps to avoid interference. FCC Monitoring Stations require an environment free of strong or spurious signals that can cause interference. The location of monitoring stations can be determined from a regional FCC office. Spread spectrum (SS) transmissions, because of their nature, have the potential to interfere with fixed frequency stations, so SS users should be sure their transmissions will not cause interference. [97.13(b), 97.303, 97.311(b)] [*General Class License Manual*, page 3-8]

G1E05 What are the restrictions on messages sent to a third party in a country with which there is a Third-Party Agreement?

A. They must relate to emergencies or disaster relief
B. They must be for other licensed amateurs
C. They must relate to amateur radio, or remarks of a personal character, or messages relating to emergencies or disaster relief
D. The message must be limited to no longer than 1 minute in duration and the name of the third party must be recorded in the station log

(C) The FCC and other licensing authorities want to prevent the amateur service from providing communications that should properly be conducted through commercial or government services. As a result, third-party communication is restricted to the types of messages in answer C. [97.115(a)(2),97.117] [*General Class License Manual*, page 3-13]

G1E06   The frequency allocations of which ITU region apply to radio amateurs operating in North and South America?

A. Region 4
B. Region 3
C. Region 2
D. Region 1

(C)   The ITU has created three administrative areas, called *regions*. Each region has its own set of frequency allocations or divisions of the radio spectrum. See **www.iaru.org/regions.html**. North and South America, Alaska, Hawaii, and most US territories and possessions are in Region 2. [97.301, ITU Radio Regulations] [*General Class License Manual*, page 3-1]

G1E07   In what part of the 2.4 GHz band may an amateur station communicate with non-licensed Wi-Fi stations?

A. Anywhere in the band
B. Channels 1 through 4
C. Channels 42 through 45
D. No part

(D)   Even if the station in primary service is using the same type of signal, amateurs in the secondary service may not contact them. [97.111] [*General Class License Manual*, page 3-8]

G1E08   What is the maximum PEP output allowed for spread spectrum transmissions?

A. 100 milliwatts
B. 10 watts
· C. 100 watts
D. 1500 watts

(B)   Since spread spectrum creates a noise-like signal that can affect other users, the output power limit for amateurs for SS signals is 10 watts. [97.313(j)] [*General Class License Manual*, page 3-15]

withdrawn

G1E09   Under what circumstances are messages that are sent via digital modes exempt from Part 97 third-party rules that apply to other modes of communication?

A. Under no circumstances
B. When messages are encrypted
C. When messages are not encrypted
D. When under automatic control

(A)   Because the messages are transmitted via Amateur Radio they must comply with all amateur rules. This means messages with commercial content or concerning business or pecuniary (financial) interests of the operator may not be transmitted via Amateur Radio. [97.115] [*General Class License Manual*, page 6-14]

G1E10 **Why should an amateur operator normally avoid transmitting on 14.100, 18.110, 21.150, 24.930 and 28.200 MHz?**

    A. A system of propagation beacon stations operates on those frequencies

    B. A system of automatic digital stations operates on those frequencies

    C. These frequencies are set aside for emergency operations

    D. These frequencies are set aside for bulletins from the FCC

(A) Amateurs should avoid transmitting on the frequencies of the system of international beacons operated by the Northern California DX Foundation (**www.ncdxf.org/beacon/**). [97.101] [*General Class License Manual*, page 3-8]

G1E11 **On what bands may automatically controlled stations transmitting RTTY or data emissions communicate with other automatically controlled digital stations?**

    A. On any band segment where digital operation is permitted

    B. Anywhere in the non-phone segments of the 10-meter or shorter wavelength bands

    C. Only in the non-phone Extra Class segments of the bands

    D. Anywhere in the 6 meter or shorter wavelength bands, and in limited segments of some of the HF bands

(D) Automatically controlled stations respond without a human control operator being present, so the FCC restricts them to certain segments of the amateur HF bands. Automatically controlled stations are permitted to contact other automatically controlled stations anywhere RTTY and data are permitted on the 6-meter and shorter wavelength bands. [97.221, 97.305] [*General Class License Manual*, page 6-14]

G1E12 When may third-party messages be transmitted via remote control?

    A. Under any circumstances in which third party messages are permitted by FCC rules

    B. Under no circumstances except for emergencies

    C. Only when the message is intended for licensed radio amateurs

    D. Only when the message is intended for third parties in areas where licensing is controlled by the FCC

(A) See G1E05. [97.115] [*General Class License Manual*, page 3-13]

Operating Procedures

[5 Exam Questions — 5 Groups]

G2A — Phone operating procedures; USB/LSB conventions; breaking into a contact; transmitter setup for voice operation; answering DX stations

G2A01 Which mode is most commonly used for voice communications on frequencies of 14 MHz or higher?

A. Upper sideband
B. Lower sideband
C. Vestigial sideband
D. Double sideband

(A) Single-sideband (SSB) modulation removes the carrier and one sideband from a double-sideband AM signal to conserve spectrum and for improved power efficiency. Amateurs normally use the upper sideband for 20 meter phone operation. Whether the upper or lower sideband is used is strictly a matter of convention and not regulated except on 60 meters where upper sideband is required. The convention to use the lower sideband on the bands below 9 MHz and the upper sideband on the higher-frequency bands developed from the design requirements of early SSB transmitters. Although modern amateur SSB equipment is more flexible, the convention persists. If everyone else on a particular band is using a certain sideband, you will need to use the same one in order to be able to communicate. [*General Class License Manual*, page 2-9]

G2A02 Which mode is most commonly used for voice communications on the 160-meter, 75-meter, and 40-meter bands?

A. Upper sideband
B. Lower sideband
C. Suppressed sideband
D. Double sideband

(B) Amateurs normally use the lower sideband for 160, 75, and 40 meter phone operation. (See also G2A01.) [*General Class License Manual*, page 2-9]

G2A03 Which mode is most commonly used for SSB voice communications in the VHF and UHF bands?

A. Upper sideband
B. Lower sideband
C. Suppressed sideband
D. Double sideband

(A) Amateurs normally use the upper sideband for VHF and UHF phone operation. (See also G2A01.) [*General Class License Manual*, page 2-9]

G2A04 Which mode is most commonly used for voice communications on the 17-meter and 12-meter bands?

A. Upper sideband
B. Lower sideband
C. Suppressed sideband
D. Double sideband

(A) Amateurs normally use the upper sideband for 17 and 12 meter phone operation. (See also G2A01.) [*General Class License Manual*, page 2-9]

G2A05 Which mode of voice communication is most commonly used on the HF amateur bands?

A. Frequency modulation
B. Double sideband
C. Single sideband
D. Phase modulation

(C) Most amateurs who use voice communications on the high frequency bands use single sideband (SSB) voice. There are some operators who prefer the high-fidelity sound of double-sideband amplitude modulation (AM). AM requires more than twice the bandwidth of an SSB signal, however. There is also some frequency modulated (FM) and phase modulated (PM) voice operation on the 10 meter band, but that mode also requires a much wider bandwidth than SSB. Some amateurs are beginning to experiment with digitally encoded voice communications, but SSB is the most common HF voice mode. [*General Class License Manual*, page 2-9]

G2A06 Which of the following is an advantage of using single sideband, as compared to other analog voice modes on the HF amateur bands?

A. Very high-fidelity voice modulation
B. Less subject to interference from atmospheric static crashes
C. Ease of tuning on receive and immunity to impulse noise
D. Less bandwidth used and greater power efficiency

(D) Single sideband (SSB) voice communication is used much more frequently than other voice modes on the HF bands because it uses less spectrum space. One sideband and the RF carrier are not transmitted with an SSB signal. That means SSB transmissions are more power efficient, since the full transmitter power is used for the remaining sideband rather than being divided between the two sidebands and carrier as it would be for AM. [*General Class License Manual*, page 2-9]

G2A07 Which of the following statements is true of the single sideband voice mode?

A. Only one sideband and the carrier are transmitted; the other sideband is suppressed
B. Only one sideband is transmitted; the other sideband and carrier are suppressed
C. SSB is the only voice mode authorized on the 20-, 15-, and 10-meter amateur bands
D. SSB is the only voice mode authorized on the 160- 75-, and 40-meter amateur bands

(B) Single sideband (SSB) voice transmissions are identified by which sideband is used. If the sideband with a frequency lower than the RF carrier frequency is used, then the signal is known as a lower sideband (LSB) transmission. If the sideband with a frequency higher than the RF carrier frequency is used, then the signal is known as an upper sideband (USB) transmission. In both cases the opposite sideband is suppressed. Amateurs normally use lower sideband on the 160, 75/80, and 40 meter bands, and upper sideband on the 20, 17, 15, 12 and 10 meter bands. This is not a requirement of the FCC Rules in Part 97, though. It is simply by common agreement. FCC Rules do, however, require amateurs to use USB on the five channels of the 60 meter band. [*General Class License Manual*, page 2-9]

G2A08   What is the recommended way to break in to a phone contact?

A. Say "QRZ" several times followed by your call sign
B. Say your call sign once
C. Say "Breaker Breaker"
D. Say "CQ" followed by the call sign of either station

(B)   Breaking into a conversation is easiest if you wait until both stations are listening so that your signal will be heard. In order to identify your transmissions during this brief period, simply state your call sign. No "over" or "break" is required, nor do you have to give either of the transmitting station's call signs. [*General Class License Manual*, page 2-5]

G2A09   Why do most amateur stations use lower sideband on the 160-, 75-, and 40-meter bands?

A. Lower sideband is more efficient than upper sideband at these frequencies
B. Lower sideband is the only sideband legal on these frequency bands
C. Because it is fully compatible with an AM detector
D. It is commonly accepted amateur practice

(D)   See G2A02. [*General Class License Manual*, page 2-9]

G2A10   Which of the following statements is true of voice VOX operation versus PTT operation?

A. The received signal is more natural sounding
B. It allows "hands free" operation
C. It occupies less bandwidth
D. It provides more power output

(B)   The purpose of a voice operated transmit (VOX) circuit is to provide automatic transmit/receive (TR) switching within an amateur station. By simply speaking into the microphone, the antenna is connected to transmitter, the receiver is muted and the transmitter is activated. When you stop speaking, the VOX circuit switches everything back to receive. Using VOX allows hands-free operation since you do not have to press a push-to-talk (PTT) switch. [*General Class License Manual*, page 2-13]

G2A11 **Generally, who should respond to a station in the contiguous 48 states who calls "CQ DX"?**

A. Any caller is welcome to respond
B. Only stations in Germany
C. Any stations outside the lower 48 states
D. Only contest stations

(C) If you hear "CQ DX" from a station on the US mainland, it usually means the CQer is looking for stations outside the lower 48 states. On the HF bands, "DX" generally refers to any station outside the caller's country. [*General Class License Manual*, page 2-5]

G2A12 **What control is typically adjusted for proper ALC setting on a single sideband transceiver?**

A. RF clipping level
B. Transmit audio or microphone gain
C. Antenna inductance or capacitance
D. Attenuator level

(B) The Automatic Level Control (ALC) circuit in a transceiver reduces microphone gain when it detects excessive power levels at the input to the RF power amplifier stages. For proper adjustment on most transmitters, the microphone gain control should be adjusted so that there is a slight movement of the ALC meter on modulation peaks. [*General Class License Manual*, page 5-8]

G2B — Operating effectively; band plans; drills and emergencies; RACES operation

G2B01 **Which of the following is true concerning access to frequencies?**

A. Nets have priority
B. QSOs in progress have priority
C. Except during emergencies, no amateur station has priority access to any frequency
D. Contest operations should yield to non-contest use of frequencies

(C) Except when the FCC has declared a communications emergency and designated specific frequencies for emergency communications, no single or group of amateurs has priority on any amateur frequency. Good operating practice is to use the flexibility of the amateur service to avoid and minimize interference. [97.101(b), (c)] [*General Class License Manual*, page 2-2]

G2B02 **What is the first thing you should do if you are communicating with another amateur station and hear a station in distress break in?**

A. Inform your local emergency coordinator

B. Acknowledge the station in distress and determine what assistance may be needed

C. Immediately decrease power to avoid interfering with the station in distress

D. Immediately cease all transmissions

(B) Whenever you hear a station in distress (where there is immediate threat to human life or property), you should take whatever action is necessary to determine what assistance that station needs and attempt to provide it. Don't assume that some other station will handle the emergency; you may be the only station receiving the distress signal. If you do hear a station in distress, the first thing you should do is to acknowledge that you heard the station, and then ask the operator where they are located and what assistance they need. [*General Class License Manual*, page 2-16]

G2B03 **What is good amateur practice if propagation changes during a contact creating interference from other stations using the frequency?**

A. Advise the interfering stations that you are on the frequency and that you have priority

B. Decrease power and continue to transmit

C. Attempt to resolve the interference problem with the other stations in a mutually acceptable manner

D. Switch to the opposite sideband

(C) Good operating practice suggests that whoever can most easily resolve an interference problem be the one to do so. If you begin to have interference from other activity on the same frequency, moving your contact to another frequency may be the simplest thing to do. Switching antennas or rotating a beam antenna may also achieve the same results. [*General Class License Manual*, page 2-4]

G2B04 **When selecting a CW transmitting frequency, what minimum separation from other stations should be used to minimize interference to stations on adjacent frequencies?**

A. 5 to 50 Hz
B. 150 to 500 Hz
C. 1 kHz to 3 kHz
D. 3 kHz to 6 kHz

(B) The more bandwidth signals occupy, the more separation is needed between contacts to avoid interference. CW emissions require the least bandwidth and need the least separation. Most radios use narrow filters for CW reception, so you should be able to select an operating frequency within about 150 to 500 Hz from another CW station without causing interference. [*General Class License Manual*, page 2-1]

G2B05 **When selecting an SSB transmitting frequency, what minimum separation should be used to minimize interference to stations on adjacent frequencies?**

A. 5 Hz to 50 Hz
B. 150 Hz to 500 Hz
C. 2 kHz to 3 kHz
D. Approximately 6 kHz

(C) The more bandwidth signals occupy, the more separation is needed between contacts to avoid interference. Single-sideband (SSB) signals use considerably more bandwidth than CW and therefore need much more separation between contacts. Under normal circumstances, you will need approximately 3 kHz of separation from another contact to avoid causing interference. [*General Class License Manual*, page 2-1]

G2B06 **How can you avoid harmful interference on an apparently clear frequency before calling CQ on CW or phone?**

A. Send "QRL?" on CW, followed by your call sign; or, if using phone, ask if the frequency is in use, followed by your call sign
B. Listen for 2 minutes before calling CQ
C. Send the letter "V" in Morse code several times and listen for a response, or say "test" several times and listen for a response
D. Send "QSY" on CW or if using phone, announce "the frequency is in use," then give your call sign and listen for a response

(A) After listening for a short period of time, if you do not hear another station transmitting on the frequency, it is good practice to make a short transmission asking if the frequency is in use. It may be that due to propagation you are unable to hear the transmitting station, but the listening station can hear you. On CQ, the Q signal "QRL?", and on phone, "Is the frequency in use?" followed by your call sign, gives the opportunity for another station to respond. [*General Class License Manual*, page 2-2]

G2B07 Which of the following complies with commonly accepted amateur practice when choosing a frequency on which to initiate a call?

A. Listen on the frequency for at least two minutes to be sure it is clear
B. Identify your station by transmitting your call sign at least 3 times
C. Follow the voluntary band plan
D. All these choices are correct

(C) Under normal conditions, following the voluntary band plan in **Table G2.1** is a good way to choose a frequency compatible with your planned type of operating. Very crowded bands or special operating events require that you be flexible in your frequency choices. [*General Class License Manual*, page 2-2]

Table G2.1
ARRL Considerate Operator's Frequency Guide for HF Bands

Frequency	Mode
160 Meters (1.8 – 2.0 MHz):	
1.800 – 2.000	CW
1.800 – 1.810	Digital Modes
1.810	QRP CW calling frequency
1.843 – 2.000	SSB, SSTV, other wideband modes
1.910	QRP SSB calling frequency
1.995 – 2.000	Experimental
1.999 – 2.000	Beacons
80 Meters (3.5 – 4.0 MHz):	
3.500 – 3.510	CW DX window
3.560	QRP CW calling frequency
3.570 – 3.600	RTTY/Data
3.585 – 3.600	Automatically controlled data stations
3.590	RTTY/Data DX
3.790 – 3.800	DX window
3.845	SSTV
3.885	AM calling frequency
3.985	QRP SSB calling frequency
40 Meters (7.0 – 7.3 MHz):	
7.030	QRP CW calling frequency
7.040	RTTY/Data DX
7.070 – 7.125	RTTY/Data
7.100 – 7.105	Automatically controlled data stations
7.171	SSTV
7.173	D-SSTV
7.285	QRP SSB calling frequency
7.290	AM calling frequency

30 Meters (10.1 – 10.15 MHz):
10.130-10.140	RTTY/Data
10.140-10.150	Automatically controlled data stations

20 Meters (14.0 – 14.35 MHz):
14.060	QRP CW calling frequency
14.070 – 14.095	RTTY/Data
14.095 – 14.0995	Automatically controlled data stations
14.100	IBP/NCDXF Beacons
14.1005 – 14.112	Automatically controlled data stations
14.230	SSTV
14.233	D-SSTV
14.236	Digital voice
14.285	QRP SSB calling frequency
14.286	AM calling frequency

17 Meters (18.068 – 18.168 MHz):
18.100 – 18.105	RTTY/Data
18.105 – 18.110	Automatically controlled data stations
18.110	IBP/NCDXF Beacons
18.162.5	Digital voice

15 Meters (21.0 – 21.45 MHz):
21.060	QRP CW calling frequency
21.070 – 21.110	RTTY/Data
21.090 – 21.100	Automatically controlled data stations
21.150	IBP/NCDXF Beacons
21.340	SSTV
21.385	QRP SSB calling frequency

12 Meters (24.89 – 24.99 MHz):
24.920 – 24.925	RTTY/Data
24.925 – 24.930	Automatically controlled data stations
24.930	IBP/NCDXF Beacons

10 Meters (28 – 29.7 MHz):
28.060	QRP CW calling frequency
28.070 – 28.120	RTTY/Data
28.120 – 28.189	Automatically controlled data stations
28.190 – 28.225	Beacons
28.200	IBP/NCDXF Beacons
28.385	QRP SSB calling frequency
28.680	SSTV
29.000-29.200	AM
29.300-29.510	Satellite Downlinks
29.520-29.590	Repeater Inputs
29.600	FM Simplex
29.610-29.700	Repeater Outputs

G2B08 What is the voluntary band plan restriction for US stations transmitting within the 48 contiguous states in the 50.1 MHz to 50.125 MHz band segment?

A. Only contacts with stations not within the 48 contiguous states
B. Only contacts with other stations within the 48 contiguous states
C. Only digital contacts
D. Only SSTV contacts

(A) DX windows were originally devised to give amateurs from countries with restricted privileges a bit of band space to make DX contacts outside their own country or region. As world-wide frequency allocations become more common, the DX windows are less needed but are still part of operating on some bands. For example, if you live in the US, the DX window of 50.1 to 50.125 MHz is where you listen for and make long-distance contacts with stations outside the contiguous 48 states. [*General Class License Manual*, page 2-5]

G2B09 Who may be the control operator of an amateur station transmitting in RACES to assist relief operations during a disaster?

A. Only a person holding an FCC-issued amateur operator license
B. Only a RACES net control operator
C. A person holding an FCC-issued amateur operator license or an appropriate government official
D. Any control operator when normal communication systems are operational

(A) The control operator of a RACES station must have an FCC-issued amateur operator license and be certified by a civil defense organization as a member. [97.407(a)] [*General Class License Manual*, page 2-16]

G2B10 Which of the following is good amateur practice for net management?

A. Always use multiple sets of phonetics during check-in
B. Have a backup frequency in case of interference or poor conditions
C. Transmit the full net roster at the beginning of every session
D. All these choices are correct

(B) For scheduled contacts and nets to run smoothly, flexibility is required from everyone. If you're the one making the schedule, avoid calling frequencies and popular band areas. If you are a net control station and find the net's chosen frequency to be occupied, find a clear frequency nearby and run the net there or change to your backup frequency. [*General Class License Manual*, page 2-5]

G2B11 How often may RACES training drills and tests be routinely conducted without special authorization?

A. No more than 1 hour per month
B. No more than 2 hours per month
C. No more than 1 hour per week
D. No more than 2 hours per week

(C) Drills and tests may not exceed a total time of 1 hour per week. With the approval of the chief officer for emergency planning the applicable State, Commonwealth, District or territory, however, such tests and drills may be conducted for a period not to exceed 72 hours no more than twice in any calendar year. [97.407(d)(4)] [*General Class License Manual*, page 2-18]

G2C — CW operating procedures and procedural signals; Q signals; full break-in

G2C01 Which of the following describes full break-in CW operation (QSK)?

A. Breaking stations send the Morse code prosign "BK"
B. Automatic keyers, instead of hand keys, are used to send Morse code
C. An operator must activate a manual send/receive switch before and after every transmission
D. Transmitting stations can receive between code characters and elements

(D) Full break-in telegraphy allows you to receive signals between your transmitted Morse code dots and dashes and between words. The advantage is that if you are making a long transmission, the receiving station can make a short transmission and get your attention. QSK is the Q signal used to describe this type of operation. [*General Class License Manual*, page 2-13]

G2C02 What should you do if a CW station sends "QRS?"

A. Send slower
B. Change frequency
C. Increase your power
D. Repeat everything twice

(A) QRS is the Q signal that means "Send slower". To ask if you should send slower, send QRS? Conversely, to increase speed, QRQ is used. [*General Class License Manual*, page 2-13]

G2C03 **What does it mean when a CW operator sends "KN" at the end of a transmission?**

A. No US stations should call
B. Operating full break-in
C. Listening only for a specific station or stations
D. Closing station now

(C) KN is an example of a CW prosign, procedural signals that help coordinate the exchange of messages and the beginning and ending of transmissions. The patterns of dots and dashes that make up prosigns are described by a pair of regular letters that, if sent together without a pause, are equivalent to the prosign. (Prosigns are often written with a line over the letters to indicate they are sent with no spaces between them as a single character.) [*General Class License Manual*, page 2-13]

G2C04 **What does the Q signal "QRL?" mean?**

A. "Will you keep the frequency clear?"
B. "Are you operating full break-in?" or "Can you operate full break-in?"
C. "Are you listening only for a specific station?"
D. "Are you busy?" or "Is this frequency in use?"

(D) QRL? is a Q signal hams use most commonly to ask if a frequency is in use before making an initial transmission. [*General Class License Manual*, page 2-2]

G2C05 **What is the best speed to use when answering a CQ in Morse code?**

A. The fastest speed at which you are comfortable copying, but no slower than the CQ
B. The fastest speed at which you are comfortable copying, but no faster than the CQ
C. At the standard calling speed of 10 wpm
D. At the standard calling speed of 5 wpm

(B) An operator calling CQ is assumed to be sending at a speed at which he or she feels comfortable receiving. Responding at a significantly higher speed is impolite and may be embarrassing to the other operator if they are unable to copy your response. If you are uncomfortable responding at the sending station's speed, send at the highest rate at which you are comfortable receiving. It is good practice to respond to calling stations at their sending speed, if it is significantly slower. [*General Class License Manual*, page 2-13]

G2C06   What does the term "zero beat" mean in CW operation?

A. Matching the speed of the transmitting station
B. Operating split to avoid interference on frequency
C. Sending without error
D. Matching the transmit frequency to the frequency of a received signal

(D)   Zero beat means to match the frequency of the transmitting station. When separate receivers and transmitters were the norm, a transmitter's frequency had to be adjusted to match the received signal's frequency. This was done by spotting — turning on the transmitter's low power stages and listening for that signal in the receiver. When the beat frequency between the desired signal and the transmitter's spotting signal reached zero frequency or zero beat, the transmitter signal and the received signal were on the same frequency. [*General Class License Manual*, page 2-13]

G2C07   When sending CW, what does a "C" mean when added to the RST report?

A. Chirpy or unstable signal
B. Report was read from an S meter rather than estimated
C. 100 percent copy
D. Key clicks

(A)   An RST with "C" appended, such as 579C, indicates that the signal is being received with chirp, a short frequency shift as the transmitter stabilizes after keying. It's a very distinctive sound and is caused by the transmitter's oscillator changing frequency when the key is closed. Chirp is often the result of low voltage from the power supply or battery. [*General Class License Manual*, page 2-11]

G2C08   **What prosign is sent to indicate the end of a formal message when using CW?**

A. SK
B. BK
C. AR
D. KN

(C)   The ARRL National Traffic System has established specific procedures for passing formal written messages by Amateur Radio. Even if you don't participate in traffic nets, it is a good idea to be familiar with the procedures for handling such messages. It can be especially helpful in an emergency for a number of reasons. By following the standard procedures it is more likely that an emergency message will be transmitted (and received) correctly. When sending formal messages using Morse code (CW), you send the message preamble, the address, message body and signature. To indicate that this is the end of the message, send the CW procedural signal (prosign) AR to show clearly that all the information has been sent. When the receiving station has accurately recorded the entire message, they will acknowledge receipt of the message by sending "QSL" or simply "R" for "received." (See also G2C03.) [*General Class License Manual*, page 2-13]

G2C09   **What does the Q signal "QSL" mean?**

A. Send slower
B. We have already confirmed by card
C. I acknowledge receipt
D. We have worked before

(C)   QSL is the Q signal that means "I acknowledge receipt". Informally, it is often used to indicate that a transmission was received and understood. QSL cards are exchanged to confirm that a contact was made. [*General Class License Manual*, page 2-13]

G2C10   **What does the Q signal "QRN" mean?**

A. Send more slowly
B. Stop sending
C. Zero beat my signal
D. I am troubled by static

(B)   QRN is the Q signal that means a station is experiencing interference from atmospheric static or noise. The related Q signal QRM refers to interference from other signals. [*General Class License Manual*, page 2-11]

G2C11 What does the Q signal "QRV" mean?

A. You are sending too fast
B. There is interference on the frequency
C. I am quitting for the day
D. I am ready to receive messages

(D) QRV is the Q signal that means "I am ready to copy" and indicates that the station with the message may begin transmitting. QRV is used whether sending formal traffic or having a regular conversation. [*General Class License Manual*, page 2-13]

G2D — Volunteer Monitoring Program; HF operations

G2D01 What is the Volunteer Monitoring Program?

A. Amateur volunteers who are formally enlisted to monitor the airwaves for rules violations
B. Amateur volunteers who conduct amateur licensing examinations
C. Amateur volunteers who conduct frequency coordination for amateur VHF repeaters
D. Amateur volunteers who use their station equipment to help civil defense organizations in times of emergency

(A) The purpose of the Volunteer Monitoring Program is to help ensure amateur self-regulation and see that amateurs follow the FCC rules properly. The Volunteer Monitoring Program volunteers deal only with amateur-to-amateur interference and improper operation. The other answer choices describe other Amateur Radio activities. Amateur volunteers who conduct licensing examinations are called Volunteer Examiners (VEs). Amateurs in charge of frequency coordination for repeaters are called Frequency Coordinators. Amateurs who help civil defense organizations in times of emergency are members of the Radio Amateur Civil Emergency Service (RACES). [*General Class License Manual*, page 3-2]

G2D02 Which of the following are objectives of the Volunteer Monitoring Program?

A. To conduct efficient and orderly amateur licensing examinations
B. To provide emergency and public safety communications
C. To coordinate repeaters for efficient and orderly spectrum usage
D. To encourage amateur radio operators to self-regulate and comply with the rules

(D) Many amateurs also volunteer to help provide emergency and public safety communications as members of ARRL's Amateur Radio Emergency Service (ARES). (See also G2D01.) [*General Class License Manual*, page 3-2]

G2D03 What procedure may be used by Volunteer Monitors to localize a station whose continuous carrier is holding a repeater on in their area?

A. Compare vertical and horizontal signal strengths on the input frequency

B. Compare beam headings on the repeater input from their home locations with that of other Volunteer Monitors

C. Compare signal strengths between the input and output of the repeater

D. All these choices are correct

(B) Friendly competitions to locate hidden transmitters, sometimes called "fox hunts" or "bunny hunts," allow participants to practice their radio direction-finding skills which are useful in locating harmful interference sources. The Volunteer Monitoring Program can use "fox hunters" to document interference cases and report them to the proper enforcement bureau. Fox hunts also make everyone aware that there is a plan in place to find and eliminate an interference source [*General Class License Manual*, page 3-2]

G2D04 Which of the following describes an azimuthal projection map?

A. A map that shows accurate land masses

B. A map that shows true bearings and distances from a specific location

C. A map that shows the angle at which an amateur satellite crosses the equator

D. A map that shows the number of degrees longitude that an amateur satellite appears to move westward at the equator with each orbit

(B) An azimuthal map, or azimuthal-equidistant projection map, is also called a great circle map (see **Figure G2.1**). When this type of map is centered on your location, a straight line shows the true direction (bearing) and shortest path to the destination. (The bearing 180 degrees different from the short-path direction shows the direction to point your antenna for long-path communications.) [*General Class License Manual*, page 7-9]

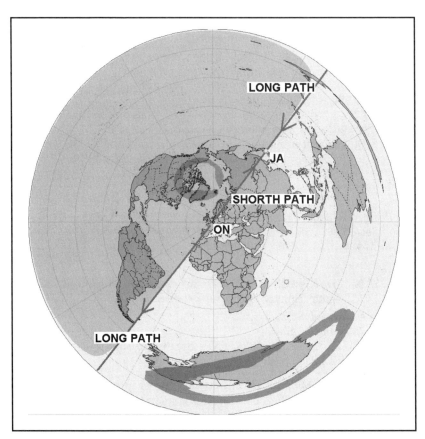

Figure G2.1 —The azimuthal or great-circle path for midwinter (0745 UTC) shows the short and the long path that exist simultaneously on 40 meters from Belgium to Japan. (Maps generated with *DX Atlas*, with additions by ON4UN.)

G2D05 **Which of the following indicates that you are looking for an HF contact with any station?**

A. Sign your call sign once, followed by the words "listening for a call" — if no answer, change frequency and repeat

B. Say "QTC" followed by "this is" and your call sign — if no answer, change frequency and repeat

C. Repeat "CQ" a few times, followed by "this is," then your call sign a few times, then pause to listen, repeat as necessary

D. Transmit an unmodulated carried for approximately 10 seconds, followed by "this is" and your call sign, and pause to listen — repeat as necessary

(C) To call CQ on phone, you say "CQ CQ CQ, this is [your call repeated a few times using phonetics]". Then pause to listen for a station responding to your CQ. If no one answers, repeat your CQ as conditions require. [*General Class License Manual*, page 2-5]

G2D06 **How is a directional antenna pointed when making a "long-path" contact with another station?**

A. Toward the rising sun

B. Along the grayline

C. 180 degrees from the station's short-path heading

D. Toward the north

(C) The shortest direct route, or great-circle path, between two points is called the short-path. If a directional antenna is pointed in exactly the opposite direction, 180 degrees different from the short-path, communications can be attempted on the long path. Long-path communication may be available when the more direct short path is closed. Because of the higher number of hops required, long path often works best when the path is across the ocean, a good reflector of HF signals. See **Figure G2.1**. [*General Class License Manual*, page 8-1]

G2D07 **Which of the following are examples of the NATO Phonetic Alphabet?**

A. Able, Baker, Charlie, Dog

B. Adam, Boy, Charles, David

C. America, Boston, Canada, Denmark

D. Alpha, Bravo, Charlie, Delta

(D) Phonetics are recommended for HF phone contacts just as they are on repeaters. The NATO phonetics (Alfa, Bravo, Charlie, Delta, and so on) are the most commonly used (see **www.arrl.org/files/file/Youth/Phonetic%20 Alphabet.pdf**. [*General Class License Manual*, page 2-2]

G2D08   Why do many amateurs keep a station log?

A. The FCC requires a log of all international contacts
B. The FCC requires a log of all international third-party traffic
C. The log provides evidence of operation needed to renew a license without retest
D. To help with a reply if the FCC requests information about your station

(D)   While useful, the FCC does not require you to keep a record (log) of your transmissions. It can be fun to keep a log, though, and then look back years later at the contacts you made. A log can also help document when your station was on the air and who was the control operator. You must give permission before a visiting amateur may operate your station. If you designate another amateur to be the control operator of your station, you both share the responsibility for the proper operation of the station. Unless your station records (log) show otherwise, the FCC will assume you were the control operator any time your station was operated. [*General Class License Manual*, page 2-5]

G2D09   Which of the following is required when participating in a contest on HF frequencies?

A. Submit a log to the contest sponsor
B. Send a QSL card to the stations worked, or QSL via Logbook of The World
C. Identify your station according to normal FCC regulations
D. All these choices are correct

(C)   The fast-paced style of contest operating is quite popular on HF. The rules for identifying your station still apply during these competitive events. [*General Class License Manual*, page 2-5]

G2D10   What is QRP operation?

A. Remote piloted model control
B. Low-power transmit operation
C. Transmission using Quick Response Protocol
D. Traffic relay procedure net operation

(B)   QRP is a Q signal that means "lower your transmitter power." Many amateurs enjoy using low power levels for the challenge, the relative simplicity of the equipment, and sometimes to reduce interference. The generally accepted level for "QRP" power is 5 watts of transmitter output on CW and 10 W PEP output on phone. [*General Class License Manual*, page 3-15]

G2D11   **Why are signal reports typically exchanged at the beginning of an HF contact?**

A. To allow each station to operate according to conditions
B. To be sure the contact will count for award programs
C. To follow standard radiogram structure
D. To allow each station to calibrate their frequency display

(A)   One of the first items of information exchanged between stations at the beginning of a contact is the signal report. This lets each station know how well their signal is being received so that they can adjust procedures according to conditions. [*General Class License Manual*, page 8-5]

G2E — Digital mode operating procedures

G2E01   **Which mode is normally used when sending RTTY signals via AFSK with an SSB transmitter?**

A. USB
B. DSB
C. CW
D. LSB

(D)   Lower sideband (LSB) is used by convention for RTTY signals on all bands except 60 meters where USB must be used. There is no technical reason why LSB is preferred over USB for RTTY signals. [*General Class License Manual*, page 6-11]

G2E02   **What is VARA?**

A. A low signal-to-noise digital mode used for EME (moonbounce)
B. A digital protocol used with Winlink
C. A radio direction finding system used on VHF and UHF
D. A DX spotting system using a network of software defined radios

(B)   Winlink is not a mode — it is a communications system. Several modes are used to access the system. If you access a Winlink mailbox station on VHF you might use regular packet radio. On HF, the PACTOR and VARA modes are used. [*General Class License Manual*, page 6-6]

G2E03 **What symptoms may result from other signals interfering with a PACTOR or VARA transmission?**

A. Frequent retries or timeouts
B. Long pauses in message transmission
C. Failure to establish a connection between stations
D. All these choices are correct

(D) Packet modes, such as PACTOR or VARA, do their best to automatically recover from reception difficulties but you should be aware of how they respond in the presence of interference. The result is generally one of these problems:

• Failure to connect — the receiver won't be able to decode your connect request and your connect attempt will fail.

• Frequent retries or transmission delays — because of the interference, your transmissions will be received with errors and the data will be garbled so your station must retransmit the data multiple times, causing the data transfer progress to be slow or erratic.

• Timeouts or dropped connections — in cases of strong or persistent interference, the number of requested retransmissions may exceed a preset limit which causes the other station to drop the connection or disconnect from your station, ending the contact. [*General Class License Manual*, page 6-14]

G2E04 **Which of the following is good practice when choosing a transmitting frequency to answer a station calling CQ using FT8?**

A. Always call on the station's frequency
B. Call on any frequency in the waterfall except the station's frequency
C. Find a clear frequency during the same time slot as the calling station
D. Find a clear frequency during the alternate time slot to the calling station

(D) Because WSJT is an open-source project, you should expect variations of FT8 to behave differently. Generally, when responding to a CQ on FT8, you should locate a clear frequency in the waterfall and select the time slot that doesn't interfere with the calling stations. Remember that time synchronization is important for FT4 and FT8. [*General Class License Manual*, page 6-6]

G2E05 **What is the standard sideband used to generate a JT65, JT9, or FT4, or FT8 digital signal when using AFSK in any amateur band?**

A. LSB
B. USB
C. DSB
D. SSB

(B) While RTTY uses LSB as the standard, JT65, JT9, and FT8 use USB. These modes are part of the WSJT-X suite of digital protocols used for meteor scatter, moonbounce (EME), and weak signal communications. [*General Class License Manual*, page 6-11]

G2E06 **What is the most common frequency shift for RTTY emissions in the amateur HF bands?**

A. 85 Hz
B. 170 Hz
C. 425 Hz
D. 850 Hz

(B) The standard audio mark and space frequencies for encoding a RTTY signal are 2125 Hz (the mark tone) and 2295 Hz (the space tone). The difference between them is called the signal's shift. The rate of shifting between mark and space tones determines the character speed. On HF, the most common speed is 60 WPM (45 baud) with a 170 Hz shift. You should always answer a RTTY station at the same speed and shift it is using. [*General Class License Manual*, page 6-4]

G2E07 **Which of the following is required when using FT8?**

A. A special hardware modem
B. Computer time accurate to within approximately 1 second
C. Receiver attenuator set to -12 dB
D. A vertically polarized antenna

(B) As the modulation and coding techniques available to amateurs become more sophisticated, they also place more demands on the computer systems used to generate and receive them. One of the requirements is a minimum level of processing speed. More processing power enables the reception of weaker signals or more signals simultaneously. Packet modes such as JT65 and FT8 also require transmissions to occur in precisely defined periods so the receiving systems know when to begin decoding. Utility software is available to keep your computer precisely synchronized to within 1 second of standard time. [*General Class License Manual*, page 6-1]

G2E08 In what segment of the 20-meter band are most digital mode operations commonly found?

A. At the bottom of the slow-scan TV segment, near 14.230 MHz
B. At the top of the SSB phone segment, near 14.325 MHz
C. In the middle of the CW segment, near 14.100 MHz
D. Between 14.070 MHz and 14.100 MHz

(D) PSK signals are generally found in the vicinity of 14.070 MHz on the 20 meter band at the bottom of the RTTY/data area listed in Table G2.2. [*General Class License Manual*, page 6-1]

G2E09 How do you join a contact between two stations using the PACTOR protocol?

A. Send broadcast packets containing your call sign while in MONITOR mode
B. Transmit a steady carrier until the PACTOR protocol times out and disconnects
C. Joining an existing contact is not possible, PACTOR connections are limited to two stations
D. Send a NAK code

(C) The PACTOR protocol is are designed to support communication between two stations so that errors can be corrected. The protocol does not support additional stations although you can monitor the communications as described in G2E02. [*General Class License Manual*, page 6-7]

Table G2.2
ARRL Band Plan for RTTY/Data Frequencies

Band (Meters)	RTTY/Data Frequencies (MHz)		
160	1.800	–	1.810
80	3.570	–	3.600
40	7.080	–	7.125
30	10.130	–	10.140
20	14.070	–	14.0995
	14.1005	–	14.112
17	18.100	–	18.105
15	21.070	–	21.110
12	24.920	–	24.925
10	28.070	–	28.150

G2E10   Which of the following is a way to establish contact with a digital messaging system gateway station?

A. Send an email to the system control operator
B. Send QRL in Morse code
C. Respond when the station broadcasts its SSID
D. Transmit a connect message on the station's published frequency

(D)   Message transfer is started by establishing a connection with the gateway station. This usually means transmitting a special "connect" message to that station on a published frequency. The gateway station usually operates without a control operator so it is up to you to make sure the channel is not being used by another station. [*General Class License Manual*, page 6-12]

G2E11   What is the primary purpose of an Amateur Radio Emergency Data Network (AREDN) mesh network?

A. To provide FM repeater coverage in remote areas
B. To provide real time propagation data by monitoring amateur radio transmissions worldwide
C. To provide high-speed data services during an emergency or community event
D. To provide DX spotting reports to aid contesters and DXers

(C)   Generally, AREDN networks are used during emergencies or to support community events like road races, parades, and other community gatherings. [*General Class License Manual*, page 6-9]

G2E12   Which of the following describes Winlink?

A. An amateur radio wireless network to send and receive email on the internet
B. A form of Packet Radio
C. A wireless network capable of both VHF and HF band operation
D. All of the above

(D)   Transferring email messages and digital files using digital modes on the HF bands has become a very common method of communication for personal and public service use. The Winlink system (**winlink.org**) has grown to a robust, worldwide packet radio system as a result. Winlink uses the internet to connect its system of email servers with gateway and mailbox stations around the world on HF, VHF, and UHF frequencies. [*General Class License Manual*, page 6-6]

G2E13 What is another name for a Winlink Remote Message Server?

A. Terminal Node Controller
B. Gateway
C. RJ-45
D. Printer/Server

(B) See the answer to question G2E12. [*General Class License Manual*, page 6-6]

G2E14 What could be wrong if you cannot decode an RTTY or other FSK signal even though it is apparently tuned in properly?

A. The mark and space frequencies may be reversed
B. You may have selected the wrong baud rate
C. You may be listening on the wrong sideband
D. All these choices are correct

(D) There a number of software configuration choices that affect how RTTY signals are decoded and displayed. The symbol rate or baud must be correct as well as the MARK and SPACE tone frequencies. You might also have your receiver set to listen on the "wrong" sideband (LSB is the RTTY standard on the HF bands) or have a "reverse shift" option selected. It is often helpful when confronting this problem to have a friend help you get started by practicing sending and receiving. [*General Class License Manual*, page 6-11]

G2E15 Which of the following is a common location for FT8?

A. Anywhere in the voice portion of the band
B. Anywhere in the CW portion of the band
C. Approximately 14.074 MHz to 14.077 MHz
D. Approximately 14.110 MHz to 14.113 MHz

(C) Digital modes such as JT65 and FT8 require transmissions to occur in precisely defined periods so the receiving systems know when to begin decoding. Utility software is available to keep your computer precisely synchronized to within 1 second of standard time. [*General Class License Manual*, page 6-6]

Radio Wave Propagation

[3 Exam Questions — 3 Groups]

G3A — Sunspots and solar radiation; geomagnectic field and stability indices

> **G3A01** How does a higher sunspot number affect HF propagation?
> A. Higher sunspot numbers generally indicate a greater probability of good propagation at higher frequencies
> B. Lower sunspot numbers generally indicate greater probability of sporadic E propagation
> C. A zero sunspot number indicates that radio propagation is not possible on any band
> D. A zero sunspot number indicates undisturbed conditions

(A)   A number of observatories around the world measure solar activity. A weighted average of this data is used to determine the International Sunspot Number (ISN) for each day. These daily sunspot counts are used to produce monthly and yearly average values. The average values are used to see trends and patterns in the measurements. See **Figure G3.1**. [*General Class License Manual*, page 8-7]

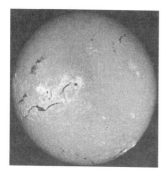

Figure G3.1 — Much more than sunspots can be seen when the sun is viewed through selective optical filters. This photo was taken through a hydrogen-alpha filter, which passes a narrow band of light wavelengths at 6562 angstroms (1 angstrom = 1×10^{-10} meters). The bright patches are active areas around and often between sunspots. Dark irregular lines are filaments of activity having no central core. Faint magnetic field lines are visible around a large central sunspot group near the disc center. [Photo courtesy of Sacramento Peak Observatory, Sunspot, New Mexico]

G3A02 **What effect does a sudden ionospheric disturbance have on the daytime ionospheric propagation?**

A. It enhances propagation on all HF frequencies
B. It disrupts signals on lower frequencies more than those on higher frequencies
C. It disrupts communications via satellite more than direct communications
D. None, because only areas on the night side of the Earth are affected

(B)   A sudden ionospheric disturbance (SID) is often the result of solar flares that release large amounts of radiation. Ultraviolet and X-ray radiation from the sun travels at the speed of light, reaching the Earth in about eight minutes. When this radiation reaches the Earth, the level of ionization in the ionosphere increases rapidly. This causes D-layer absorption of radio waves to increase significantly. Absorption of radio signals in the D layer is always stronger at lower frequencies, affecting lower frequency signals more than higher frequency signals. [*General Class License Manual*, page 8-9]

G3A03 **Approximately how long does it take the increased ultraviolet and X-ray radiation from a solar flare to affect radio propagation on Earth?**

A. 28 days
B. 1 to 2 hours
C. 8 minutes
D. 20 to 40 hours

(C)   Ultraviolet and X-ray radiation from the sun travels at the speed of light, reaching the Earth in about eight minutes (see **Figure G3.2**). [*General Class License Manual*, page 8-9]

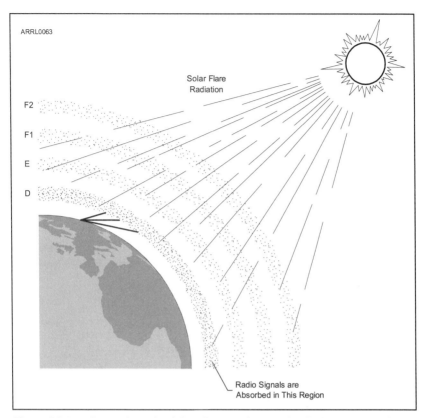

ARRL0063

Solar Flare
Radiation

F2

F1

E

D

Radio Signals are
Absorbed in This Region

Figure G3.2 — Approximately eight minutes after a solar flare occurs on the sun, the ultraviolet and X-ray radiation released by the flare reaches the Earth. This radiation causes increased ionization and radio-wave absorption in the D region of the ionosphere.

G3A04   **Which of the following are the least reliable bands for long-distance communications during periods of low solar activity?**

A.   80 meters and 160 meters
B.   60 meters and 40 meters
C.   30 meters and 20 meters
D.   15 meters, 12 meters, and 10 meters

(D)   The higher the frequency, the more ionization is needed in the ionosphere in order to refract (bend) the radio signal back to the Earth. When solar activity is low, signals at higher frequencies will pass through the ionosphere into space instead of being refracted back to Earth. During periods of low solar activity, the 15 meter (21 MHz), 12 meter (24.9 MHz) and 10 meter (28 MHz) bands are the least reliable HF bands for long distance communication. [*General Class License Manual*, page 8-7]

G3A05   What is the solar flux index?

   A. A measure of the highest frequency that is useful for ionospheric propagation between two points on Earth
   B. A count of sunspots that is adjusted for solar emissions
   C. Another name for the American sunspot number
   D. A measure of solar radiation at 10.7 centimeters wavelength

(D)   Solar flux is the radio energy coming from the sun. High levels of solar energy produce greater ionization in the ionosphere. The solar flux measurement is taken daily by measuring radio energy from the sun at 2800 MHz which is a wavelength of 10.7 cm. The measurement is then converted into the solar flux index. Higher values of the solar flux index correspond to higher values of solar flux. The solar-flux measurement may be taken under any weather conditions — the sun does not have to be visible, as for determining the sunspot number. The radio energy measurement is converted to an open-ended numeric index with a minimum value of 65 (for the minimum amount of energy). Higher values of the solar flux index indicate higher levels of solar activity [*General Class License Manual*, page 8-7]

G3A06   What is a geomagnetic storm?

   A. A sudden drop in the solar flux index
   B. A thunderstorm that affects radio propagation
   C. Ripples in the geomagnetic force
   D. A temporary disturbance in Earth's geomagnetic field

(D)   Geomagnetic disturbances result when charged particles from a solar flare reach the Earth. When these charged particles reach the Earth's magnetic field, they are deflected toward the North and South poles. Radio communications along higher-latitude paths (latitudes greater than about 45 degrees) will be more affected than paths closer to the equator. The charged particles from the sun may make the F-region seem to disappear or seem to split into many layers, degrading or completely blacking out long-distance radio communications. [*General Class License Manual*, page 8-9]

G3A07   At what point in the solar cycle does the 20-meter band usually support worldwide propagation during daylight hours?

   A. At the summer solstice
   B. Only at the maximum point
   C. Only at the minimum point
   D. At any point

(D)   Even at the minimum point of the solar cycle, world-wide propagation is usually possible on the 20 meter band. As solar activity increases, the band will remain open for longer periods and with stronger signal strengths. For this reason, 20 meters is a favorite band for "DXers." [*General Class License Manual*, page 8-7]

G3A08 How can an a geomagnetic storm affect HF propagation?

A. Improve high-latitude HF propagation
B. Degrade ground wave propagation
C. Improve ground wave propagation
D. Degraded high-latitude HF propagation

(D) See G3A06. [*General Class License Manual*, page 8-9]

G3A09 How can high geomagnetic activity benefit radio communications?

A. Creates auroras that can reflect VHF signals
B. Increases signal strength for HF signals passing through the polar regions
C. Improve HF long path propagation
D. Reduce long delayed echoes

(A) Auroras are actually the glow of gases ionized by the incoming charged particles as they flow vertically down into the atmosphere, guided by the Earth's magnetic field. The resulting conductive sheets that light up the night sky also reflect radio waves above 20 MHz. In particular, auroral propagation is strongest on 6 and 2 meters, modulating the signals with a characteristic hiss or buzz. [*General Class License Manual*, page 8-9]

G3A10 What causes HF propagation conditions to vary periodically in a 26- to 28-day cycle?

A. Long term oscillations in the upper atmosphere
B. Cyclic variation in Earth's radiation belts
C. Rotation of the Sun's surface layers around its axis
D. The position of the Moon in its orbit

(C) It takes approximately 28 days for the sun to rotate on its axis. Since active areas on the sun may persist for more than one rotation, you can expect similar propagation conditions to recur approximately every 28 days. [*General Class License Manual*, page 8-7]

G3A11 How long does it take a coronal mass ejection to affect radio propagation on Earth?

A. 28 days
B. 14 days
C. 4 to 8 minutes
D. 15 hours to several days

(D) Plasma, charged particles, and other material from coronal holes and coronal mass ejections from the sun travels at speeds of two million miles per hour or more, so it can take 15 to 40 hours for the plasma to travel the 93 million miles to Earth. [*General Class License Manual*, page 8-9]

G3A12   What does the K-index measure?

A. The relative position of sunspots on the surface of the Sun
B. The short-term stability of Earth's magnetic field
C. The stability of the Sun's magnetic field
D. The solar radio flux at Boulder, Colorado

(B)   K values from 0 to 9 represent the short-term stability of the Earth's magnetic or geomagnetic field, updated every three hours at the National Institute of Standards and Technology (NIST) in Boulder, Colorado. Steady values indicate a stable geomagnetic field. Higher values indicate that the geomagnetic field is disturbed, which disrupts HF communications. [*General Class License Manual*, page 8-7]

G3A13   What does the A-index measure?

A. The relative position of sunspots on the surface of the Sun
B. The amount of polarization of the Sun's electric field
C. The long-term stability of Earth's geomagnetic field
D. The solar radio flux at Boulder, Colorado

(C)   The A-index is based on the previous eight K index values from around the world. The A index gives a good picture of long-term geomagnetic field stability. Values range from 0 (stable) to 400 (greatly disturbed). [*General Class License Manual*, page 8-7]

G3A14   How is long distance radio communication usually affected by the charged particles that reach Earth from solar coronal holes?

A. HF communication is improved
B. HF communication is disturbed
C. VHF/UHF ducting is improved
D. VHF/UHF ducting is disturbed

(B)   The corona is the sun's outer layer. Temperatures in the corona are typically about two million degrees Celsius, but can be more than four million degrees Celsius above an active sunspot region. A coronal hole is an area of somewhat lower temperature. Matter ejected through such a "hole" is in the form of plasma, a highly ionized gas made up of electrons, protons and neutral particles. If the "jet" of material is directed toward the Earth it can result in a geomagnetic storm on Earth, disrupting HF communications. [*General Class License Manual*, page 8-9]

G3B — Maximum Usable Frequency; Lowest Usable Frequency; short path and long path propagation; determining propagation conditions; ionospheric refraction

G3B01   What is a characteristic of skywave signals arriving at your location by both short-path and long-path propagation?

A. Periodic fading approximately every 10 seconds
B. Signal strength increased by 3 dB
C. The signal might be cancelled causing severe attenuation
D. A slightly delayed echo might be heard

(D)   Occasionally, propagation over both the long and short paths will be supported. Unless the long and short paths are almost equal (such as between stations located at each other's antipode) there will be an echo as the more delayed signal arrives a fraction of a second later. Occasionally, round-the-world propagation is supported and you can hear your own signal coming all the way around to your location about 1/7 of a second later! [*General Class License Manual*, page 8-1]

G3B02   What factors affect the MUF?

A. Path distance and location
B. Time of day and season
C. Solar radiation and ionospheric disturbances
D. All these choices are correct

(D)   Maximum Usable Frequency (MUF) is the highest frequency that will provide skywave propagation between two specific locations. Different distances and directions will often result in very different MUF values. The MUF depends on conditions in the ionosphere, and those conditions will vary by time of day as well as the season of the year. The amount of solar radiation striking the ionosphere (see **Figure G3.3**) varies significantly depending on the timing of the 11-year sunspot cycle. Any solar flares, coronal-mass ejections and other disturbances on the sun can also result in ionospheric disturbances that will affect the MUF. [*General Class License Manual*, page 8-9]

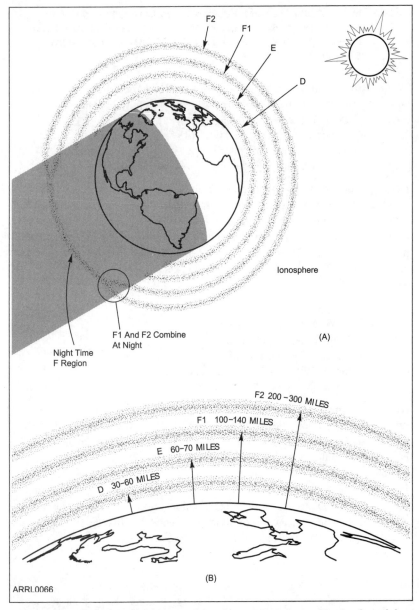

Figure G3.3 — The ionosphere consists of several regions of ionized particles at different heights above the Earth. At night, the D and E regions disappear and the F1 and F2 regions combine to form a single F region.

G3B03   Which frequency will have the least attenuation for long-distance skip propagation?

A. Just below the MUF
B. Just above the LUF
C. Just below the critical frequency
D. Just above the critical frequency

(A)   Ionospheric absorption (attenuation) is lowest just below the Maximum Usable Frequency (MUF). Use a frequency just below the MUF for the highest received signal strength. (See also G3B05.) [*General Class License Manual*, page 8-9]

G3B04   Which of the following is a way to determine current propagation on a desired band from your station?

A. Use a network of automated receiving stations on the internet to see where your transmissions are being received
B. Check the A-index
C. Send a series of dots and listen for echoes
D. All these choices are correct

(A)   Beacon stations transmit signals so that amateur operators can evaluate propagation conditions. For example, by listening for beacon stations from Western Europe, you will be able to determine if the MUF is high enough for 10 meter communications to that area. (See also G3B05.) [*General Class License Manual*, page 8-9]

G3B05   How does the ionosphere affect radio waves with frequencies below the MUF and above the LUF?

A. They are refracted back to Earth
B. They pass through the ionosphere
C. They are amplified by interaction with the ionosphere
D. They are refracted and trapped in the ionosphere to circle Earth

(A)   The MUF is the highest frequency that will allow the radio wave to reach its desired destination using E or F-region propagation. There is no single MUF for a given transmitter location; it will vary depending on the direction and distance to the station you are attempting to contact. Signals at frequencies lower than the MUF are generally bent back to Earth, while those higher than the MUF will pass through the ionosphere instead of being bent back to the Earth. The LUF specifies the lowest frequency for which propagation exists between two points. Waves below the LUF will be completely absorbed by the ionosphere. To make contact with a distant station, you will have to use a frequency between the LUF and the MUF so the wave is bent back to Earth but isn't absorbed. If the MUF drops below the LUF, then no propagation exists between those two points via ordinary skywave. See **Figure G3.4**. [*General Class License Manual*, page 8-10]

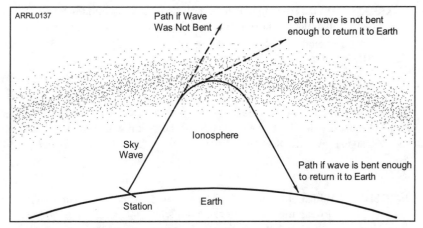

Figure G3.4 — Radio waves are bent in the ionosphere, so they return to Earth far from the transmitter. If the radio wave is not bent (refracted) enough in the ionosphere, it will pass into space rather than returning to Earth.

G3B06   **What usually happens to radio waves with frequencies below the LUF?**

A. They are refracted back to Earth
B. They pass through the ionosphere
C. They are attenuated before reaching the destination
D. They are refracted and trapped in the ionosphere to circle Earth

(C)   See G3B05. [*General Class License Manual*, page 8-10]

G3B07   **What does LUF stand for?**

A. The Lowest Usable Frequency for communications between two specific points
B. Lowest Usable Frequency for communications to any point outside a 100-mile radius
C. The Lowest Usable Frequency during a 24-hour period
D. Lowest Usable Frequency during the past 60 minutes

(A)   See G3B05. [*General Class License Manual*, page 8-10]

G3B08   **What does MUF stand for?**

A. The Minimum Usable Frequency for communications between two points
B. The Maximum Usable Frequency for communications between two points
C. The Minimum Usable Frequency during a 24-hour period
D. The Maximum Usable Frequency during a 24-hour period

(B)   See G3B05. [*General Class License Manual*, page 8-10]

G3B09 What is the approximate maximum distance along the Earth's surface normally covered in one hop using the F2 region?

A. 180 miles
B. 1,200 miles
C. 2,500 miles
D. 12,000 miles

(C) Layers in the F region form and decay in correlation with the daily passage of the sun. The F1 and F2 layers form when the F region splits into two parts due to high radiation from the sun, recombining into a single F layer at night. The more solar radiation the F region receives, the more it is ionized so it reaches maximum ionization shortly after noon during the summertime. The ionization tapers off very gradually towards sunset and the F2 layer remains usable into the night. The F2 region is the highest of the ionosphere, reaching as high as 300 miles at noon in the summertime. Because it is the highest, it is the region mainly responsible for long-distance communications. A one-hop transmission can travel a maximum distance of about 2,500 miles using F2 propagation. See **Figure G3.5**. [*General Class License Manual*, page 8-1]

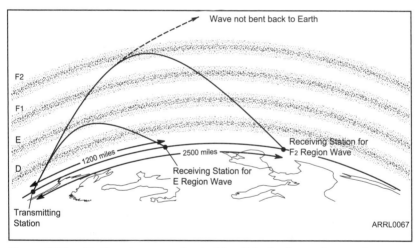

Figure G3.5 — Radio waves are refracted (bent) in the ionosphere and may return to Earth. If the radio waves are refracted to Earth from the F2 region, they may return to Earth about 2,500 miles from the transmitting station. If the radio waves are refracted to Earth from the E region, they may return to Earth about 1,200 miles from the transmitting station.

G3B10 **What is the approximate maximum distance along the Earth's surface normally covered in one hop using the E region?**

A. 180 miles
B. 1,200 miles
C. 2,500 miles
D. 12,000 miles

(B) The E region of the ionosphere is the second lowest, just above the D region. The E layer forms at an altitude of about 70 miles above the Earth. The E region ionizes during the daytime, but does not stay ionized very long after sunset. Ionization in the E region is at a maximum around midday. During the daytime, a radio signal can travel a maximum distance of about 1,200 miles in one hop using E-region propagation. [*General Class License Manual*, page 8-1]

G3B11 **What happens to HF propagation when the LUF exceeds the MUF?**

A. Propagation via ordinary skywave communications is not possible over that path
B. HF communications over the path are enhanced
C. Double-hop propagation along the path is more common
D. Propagation over the path on all HF frequencies is enhanced

(A) See G3B05. [*General Class License Manual*, page 8-10]

G3B12 **Which of the following is typical of the lower HF frequencies during the summer?**

A. Poor propagation at any time of day
B. World-wide propagation during daylight hours
C. Heavy distortion on signals due to photon absorption
D. High levels of atmospheric noise or static

(D) There are strong daily and seasonal variations in HF propagation at any point in the sunspot cycle. The seasons also affect propagation as the hemispheres receive more or less solar illumination. In summer, the higher illumination and absorption make daytime HF propagation more difficult, driving up atmospheric noise and static, shifting activity toward the evenings. The opposite happens in the winter. Propagation around the equinoxes in March and September can be very interesting at any time of the sunspot cycle. [General Class License Manual, page 8-7]

G3C — Ionospheric regions; critical angle and frequency; HF scatter; near vertical incidence skywave (NVIS)

G3C01   Which ionospheric region is closest to the surface of Earth?

A. The D region
B. The E region
C. The F1 region
D. The F2 region

(A)   The D region of the ionosphere is the lowest, forming the D layer at a height of 30 to 60 miles. Because it is the lowest, it is also the densest and its ionization disappears by dark. [*General Class License Manual*, page 8-1]

G3C02   What is meant by the term "critical frequency" at a given incidence angle?

A. The highest frequency which is refracted back to Earth
B. The lowest frequency which is refracted back to Earth
C. The frequency at which the signal-to-noise ratio approaches unity
D. The frequency at which the signal-to-noise ratio is 6 dB

(A)   Some combinations of frequency and ionization level result in weak bending. In these cases, the wave must leave the Earth's surface at a low enough angle for the bending of the wave to send it back. The highest takeoff angle at which a wave can be returned to Earth is the critical angle. If the wave enters the ionosphere at a steeper angle, it might be diffracted, but not enough to return it to Earth, and it is lost to space. The critical angle depends on ionospheric conditions and frequency. The companion to critical angle is critical frequency, the highest frequency on which a wave transmitted straight up will be returned to Earth. Measuring the critical frequency with ionosonde equipment gives the height of all the ionosphere's regions and helps provide a day-to-day picture of the ionosphere's status and activity. (An ionosonde is a special type of radar instrument for measuring ionospheric parameters.) [*General Class License Manual*, page 8-1]

G3C03   Why is skip propagation via the F2 region longer than that via the other ionospheric regions?

A. Because it is the densest
B. Because of the Doppler effect
C. Because it is the highest
D. Because of temperature inversions

(C)   Because the F2 region is the highest ionospheric region, it is the region mainly responsible for long-distance communications. A signal can travel a maximum distance of about 2,500 miles via one-hop from the F2 region. [*General Class License Manual*, page 8-1]

G3C04 **What does the term "critical angle" mean, as applied to radio wave propagation?**

A. The long path azimuth of a distant station
B. The short path azimuth of a distant station
C. The lowest takeoff angle that will return a radio wave to Earth under specific ionospheric conditions
D. The highest takeoff angle that will return a radio wave to Earth under specific ionospheric conditions

(D) See **G3C02** and **Figure G3.6**. [*General Class License Manual*, page 8-2]

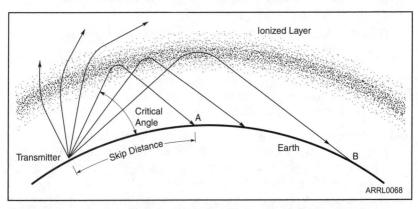

Figure G3.6 — Radio waves that leave the transmitting antenna at an angle higher than the critical angle are not refracted enough to return to Earth. A radio wave at the critical angle will return to Earth. The lowest-angle wave will return to Earth farther away than the wave at the critical angle. This illustrates the importance of low radiation angles for working DX.

G3C05 Why is long-distance communication on the 40-, 60-, 80-, and 160-meter bands more difficult during the day?

A. The F region absorbs signals at these frequencies during daylight hours
B. The F region is unstable during daylight hours
C. The D region absorbs signals at these frequencies during daylight hours
D. The E region is unstable during daylight hours

(C) Think of the D region as the Darned Daylight region. Instead of bending HF signals back to Earth, it absorbs energy from them. Signals at lower frequencies (longer wavelengths such as 160, 80, 60 and 40 meters) are absorbed more than at higher frequencies. The ionization created by the sunlight does not last very long in the D region, disappearing at or shortly after sunset. See **Figure G3.7**. [*General Class License Manual*, page 8-2]

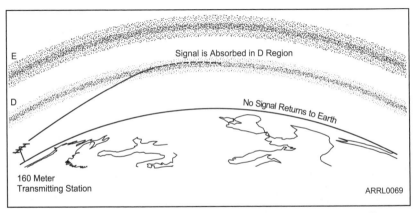

Figure G3.7 — The D region of the ionosphere absorbs energy from radio waves. Lower-frequency radio waves don't make it all the way through the D region, so the waves do not return to Earth. Higher-frequency waves travel through the D region, and are then refracted (bent) back to Earth.

G3C06 What is a characteristic of HF scatter?

A. Phone signals have high intelligibility
B. Signals have a fluttering sound
C. There are very large, sudden swings in signal strength
D. Scatter propagation occurs only at night

(B) The area between the farthest reach of ground-wave propagation and the point where signals are refracted back from the ionosphere (skywave propagation) is called the skip zone. Since some of the transmitted signal is scattered in the atmosphere or from ground reflections, communication may be possible in the skip zone by the use of scatter signals. The amount of signal scattered in the atmosphere will be quite small and the signal received in the skip zone will arrive from several paths. This tends to produce a weak, distorted signal with a fluttering or wavering sound. See **Figure G3.8**. [*General Class License Manual*, page 8-12]

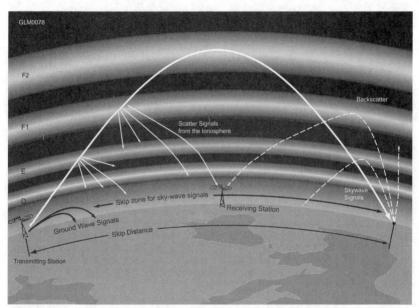

Figure G3.8 — Radio waves may be reflected back towards the transmitting station from variations in the ionosphere or after striking the ground after ionospheric reflection. Some of this energy may be scattered back into the skip zone as a weak, highly variable signal.

G3C07 What makes HF scatter signals often sound distorted?

A. The ionospheric region involved is unstable
B. Ground waves are absorbing much of the signal
C. The E region is not present
D. Energy is scattered into the skip zone through several different paths

(D) The amount of signal scattered back toward the transmitting station from the ionosphere or ground will be quite small. The signal received in the skip zone will also arrive from several radio-wave paths. This tends to produce a weak, distorted signal with a fluttering or wavering sound. (See also G3C06.) [*General Class License Manual*, page 8-12]

G3C08 Why are HF scatter signals in the skip zone usually weak?

A. Only a small part of the signal energy is scattered into the skip zone
B. Signals are scattered from the magnetosphere, which is not a good reflector
C. Propagation is via ground waves, which absorb most of the signal energy
D. Propagation is via ducts in the F region, which absorb most of the energy

(A) See G3C07. [*General Class License Manual*, page 8-12]

G3C09 What type of propagation allows signals to be heard in the transmitting station's skip zone?

A. Faraday rotation
B. Scatter
C. Chordal hop
D. Short-path

(B) The area between the farthest reach of ground-wave propagation and the point where signals are refracted back from the ionosphere (skywave propagation) is called the skip zone. Since some of the transmitted signal is scattered in the atmosphere, communication may be possible in the skip zone by the use of scatter signals. (See also G3C06.) [*General Class License Manual*, page 8-12]

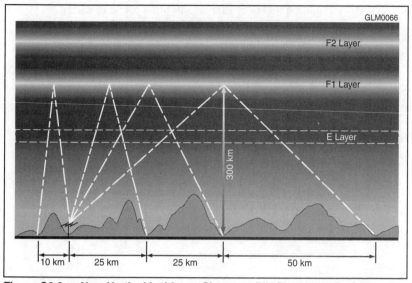

Figure G3.9 — Near Vertical Incidence Sky-wave (NVIS) communications relies on signals below the critical frequency transmitted at high vertical angles. The signals are reflected by the ionosphere back to Earth in the region around the transmitter.

G3C10 What is near vertical incidence skywave (NVIS) propagation?

    A. Propagation near the MUF
    B. Short distance MF or HF propagation at high elevation angles
    C. Long path HF propagation at sunrise and sunset
    D. Double hop propagation near the LUF

(B)　　Near vertical incidence skywave (NVIS) propagation refers to communication using skywave signals transmitted at very high vertical angles. The frequencies used are below the critical frequency, meaning that their critical angle (see question G3C02) is ninety degrees, meaning they can be reflected straight back down to Earth. Because the signals travel at high angles, they have a minimum amount of attenuation from the D and E layers. The result is good communications in a region around the transmitter over distances higher than supported by ground-wave propagation. See **Figure G3.9**. [*General Class License Manual*, page 8-12]

G3C11 Which ionospheric region is the most absorbent of signals below 10 MHz during daylight hours?

    A. The F2 region
    B. The F1 region
    C. The E region
    D. The D region

(D)　　See G3C05. [*General Class License Manual*, page 8-2]

Amateur Radio Practices

[5 Exam Questions — 5 groups]

G4A — Station configuration and operation

G4A01 What is the purpose of the notch filter found on many HF transceivers?

A. To restrict the transmitter voice bandwidth
B. To reduce interference from carriers in the receiver passband
C. To eliminate receiver interference from impulse noise sources
D. To remove interfering splatter generated by signals on adjacent frequencies

(B) A notch filter removes a very narrow band of frequencies — the "notch" — from its input. This allows the notch filter to get rid of an interfering tone, such as from an unmodulated carrier, while maintaining the intelligibility of the desired signal. An automatic notch filter can detect the presence of steady tones and remove them without operator intervention. [*General Class License Manual*, page 5-16]

G4A02 What is the benefit of using the opposite or "reverse" sideband when receiving CW?

A. Interference from impulse noise will be eliminated
B. More stations can be accommodated within a given signal passband
C. It may be possible to reduce or eliminate interference from other signals
D. Accidental out-of-band operation can be prevented

(C) Interference from nearby signals can often be avoided by switching the receiver's carrier frequency to the opposite side of the desired signal, without changing its audio pitch. This won't work on SSB because it also inverts the spectrum of the speech, rendering it unintelligible. [*General Class License Manual*, page 5-16]

G4A03   How does a noise blanker work?

A. By temporarily increasing received bandwidth
B. By redirecting noise pulses into a filter capacitor
C. By reducing receiver gain during a noise pulse
D. By clipping noise peaks

(C)   Most receivers also provide noise blankers and noise reduction features. Noise blankers operate by sensing short, sharp pulses in the IF signals and quickly reducing the gain of IF and audio amplifiers during the pulse. This is called "blanking." If the noise blanker is adjustable, it can be set to blank the receiver at different levels of noise. Noise blankers can confuse strong signals elsewhere on a band for a noise pulse, causing distortion of desired signals. This distortion can be minimized by using the minimum amount of blanking necessary or turning off the noise blanker entirely.   page 5-16]

G4A04   What is the effect on plate current of the correct setting of a vacuum-tube RF power amplifier's TUNE control?

A. A pronounced peak
B. A pronounced dip
C. No change will be observed
D. A slow, rhythmic oscillation

(B)   See G4A08. [*General Class License Manual*, page 5-14]

G4A05   Why is automatic level control (ALC) used with an RF power amplifier?

A. To balance the transmitter audio frequency response
B. To reduce harmonic radiation
C. To prevent excessive drive
D. To increase overall efficiency

(C)   The ALC circuit of an RF power amplifier senses the amount of input power and generates a feedback voltage to keep the transmitter from generating too much power for the amplifier input. This helps prevent spurious emissions that cause interference to other stations. Note that ALC should not be used with digital signals since it can result in distortion of the signal's waveform. [*General Class License Manual*, page 5-14]

G4A06 **What is the purpose of an antenna tuner?**
A. Reduce the SWR in the feed line to the antenna
B. Reduce the power dissipation in the feedline to the antenna
C. Increase power transfer from the transmitter to the feed line
D. All these choices are correct

(C) There are many names for devices that use LC circuits to convert one impedance to another — antenna coupler, impedance matching unit, transmatch, and antenna tuner are common. Remember that an "antenna tuner" does not tune the antenna at all — it only changes the impedance of your antenna system at the end of the feed line to match that of your transmitter, or put another way, an antenna tuner increases the power transfer from the transmitter to the feed line. [*General Class License Manual*, page 7-19]

G4A07 **What happens as a receiver's noise reduction control level is increased?**
A. Received signals may become distorted
B. Received frequency may become unstable
C. CW signals may become severely attenuated
D. Received frequency may shift several kHz

(A) Noise reduction is performed on the receiver's output audio by DSP. This system attempts to remove hiss and noise from the audio that is not part of the desired speech, data, or CW. There may be more than one noise reduction setting optimized for different types of signals. Increasing the noise reduction level may cause some of the desired signal to be removed as well, causing distortion. Use the least noise reduction required to minimize distortion. [*General Class License Manual*, page 5-14]

G4A08 **What is the correct adjustment for the LOAD or COUPLING control of a vacuum tube RF power amplifier?**
A. Minimum SWR on the antenna
B. Minimum plate current without exceeding maximum allowable grid current
C. Highest plate voltage while minimizing grid current
D. Desired power output without exceeding maximum allowable plate current

(D) The TUNE control of a vacuum tube RF amplifier sets the impedance matching circuit to resonance at the frequency of operation. With transmitter power applied, the TUNE control is adjusted until a pronounced dip in plate current indicates that the circuit is resonant at the operating frequency. The LOAD or COUPLING control is then used to adjust the amount of output power. The TUNE and LOAD controls are alternately adjusted until the required amount of output power is obtained without exceeding the tube's plate current rating. [*General Class License Manual*, page 5-14]

G4A09 **What is the purpose of delaying RF output after activating a transmitter's keying line to an external amplifier?**

A. To prevent key clicks on CW
B. To prevent transient overmodulation
C. To allow time for the amplifier to switch the antenna between the transceiver and the amplifier output
D. To allow time for the amplifier power supply to reach operating level

(C) If a relay switches while RF is present in the circuit that is called hot switching. At high power levels hot switching can damage the relay, so it is important to let the relay complete switching before energizing the circuit. Similarly, it is important to disconnect sensitive receive circuits before transmitter RF is enabled. A controlled time delay, called sequencing is used to ensure that all relay and switching operations are completed before enabling the transmitter. [*General Class License Manual*, page 5-14]

G4A10 **What is the function of an electronic keyer?**

A. Automatic transmit/receive switching
B. Automatic generation of dots and dashes for CW operation
C. To allow time for switching the antenna from the receiver to the transmitter
D. Computer interface for PSK and RTTY operation

(B) Electronic keyers eliminate a lot of the manual work involved in operating a straight key and ensure that each dot or dash has the right length and spacing. This allows comfortable high-speed Morse operation even for extended periods of time. [*General Class License Manual*, page 2-13]

G4A11 **Why should the ALC system be inactive when transmitting AFSK data signals?**

A. ALC will invert the modulation of the AFSK mode
B. The ALC action distorts the signal
C. When using digital modes, too much ALC activity can cause the transmitter to overheat
D. All these choices are correct

(B) ALC circuits reduce gain when power levels get too high so that higher amplitude input signals are amplified less than low ones. In effect, this compresses the signal similarly to how a speech processor works. For a voice signal, the resulting distortion is an acceptable trade for the higher average power because your ears can make up the difference. For a digital signal, however, the distortion caused by ALC makes the signal harder to decode and creates spurious emissions just like overmodulation does. [*General Class License Manual*, page 6-12]

G4A12   Which of the following is a common use of the dual-VFO feature on a transceiver?

A. To allow transmitting on two frequencies at once
B. To permit full duplex operation -- that is, transmitting and receiving at the same time
C. To transmit on one frequency and listen on another
D. To improve frequency accuracy by allowing variable frequency output (VFO) operation

(C)   Dual VFOs are used for split operation where it can be very useful to listen to the DX station's transmit and receive frequencies. Another use for dual VFOs is to monitor one frequency continuously while operating on another frequency. (See also G4A03.) [*General Class License Manual*, page 2-2]

G4A13   What is the purpose of using a receive attenuator?

A. To prevent receiver overload from strong incoming signals
B. To reduce the transmitter power when driving a linear amplifier
C. To reduce power consumption when operating from batteries
D. To reduce excessive audio level on strong signals

(A)   Too strong an input signal can overload a receiver, creating distortion products that interfere with reception of the desired signal. Using an attenuator reduces the input signal level and potential receiver overload. [*General Class License Manual*, page 5-16]

G4B — Tests and test equipment

G4B01   What item of test equipment contains horizontal and vertical channel amplifiers?

A. An ohmmeter
B. A signal generator
C. An ammeter
D. An oscilloscope

(D)   An analog oscilloscope uses one signal to deflect a beam of electrons horizontally across the face of the screen and a second signal to deflect them vertically. The electron beam causes a phosphor coating on the inside of the screen to glow so that the beam's position, representing the input signal voltages, can be observed. Digital oscilloscopes convert the signals to data and display it on a computer-like screen to show voltages in the same way. Some oscilloscopes also accept a second input signal which allows two signals to be compared to each other at the same time. [*General Class License Manual*, page 4-42]

G4B02 Which of the following is an advantage of an oscilloscope versus a digital voltmeter?

A. An oscilloscope uses less power
B. Complex impedances can be easily measured
C. Greater precision
D. Complex waveforms can be measured

(D) Digital voltmeters display measured values of voltage with excellent precision but they cannot measure a complex signal waveform's time-related behavior, such as frequency, or how it reacts to other signals. [*General Class License Manual*, page 4-42]

G4B03 Which of the following is the best instrument to use for checking the keying waveform of a CW transmitter?

A. An oscilloscope
B. A field strength meter
C. A sidetone monitor
D. A wavemeter

(A) An oscilloscope visually displays a signal waveform. This allows you to observe the shape of the CW signal's rise and fall time of the signal and the shape of signal's envelope. It also allows you to observe problems such as flat-topping (caused by overmodulation) on your SSB signal. [*General Class License Manual*, page 4-42]

G4B04 What signal source is connected to the vertical input of an oscilloscope when checking the RF envelope pattern of a transmitted signal?

A. The local oscillator of the transmitter
B. An external RF oscillator
C. The transmitter balanced mixer output
D. The attenuated RF output of the transmitter

(D) When the RF output from a transmitter is connected to the vertical channel of an oscilloscope, the oscilloscope visually displays the signal's envelope. This allows you to check for signal distortion such as flat-topping (caused by overmodulation). Use an attenuator or RF sampling device to limit the voltage at the oscilloscope input. [*General Class License Manual*, page 4-43]

G4B05   Why do voltmeters have high input impedance?

A. It improves the frequency response
B. It allows for higher voltages to be safely measured
C. It improves the resolution of the readings
D. It decreases the loading on circuits being measured

(D)   The higher the impedance of a voltmeter, the smaller the amount of current drawn from the circuit being tested. This allows the voltmeter to make an accurate measurement of voltage while disturbing the circuit as little as possible. [*General Class License Manual*, page 4-43]

G4B06   What is an advantage of a digital multimeter as compared to an analog voltmeter?

A. Better for measuring computer circuits
B. Less prone to overload
C. Higher precision
D. Faster response

(C)   A digital voltmeter or multimeter displays measurements of voltage, current and resistance in numeric form instead of using a moving needle and a fixed scale. That results in significantly better precision than an analog meter. Analog meters, however, may be a better choice for adjusting a circuit for maximum and minimum values because the needle movement is easier to see than it is to evaluate changes of a numeric display. [*General Class License Manual*, page 4-43]

G4B07   What signals are used to conduct a two-tone test?

A. Two audio signals of the same frequency shifted 90 degrees
B. Two non-harmonically related audio signals
C. Two swept frequency tones
D. Two audio frequency range square wave signals of equal amplitude

(B)   On AM or SSB, a two-tone test can be used to monitor transmitter linearity. This test consists of modulating your transmitter with a pair of audio tones that are not harmonically related (700 and 1900 Hz are typical frequencies) while watching the transmitted signal on a monitoring oscilloscope. The transmitter and any external amplifier are then adjusted for an output free of distortion. This test needs only to be performed occasionally to note the appropriate settings of gain and level adjustments. [*General Class License Manual*, page 5-8]

G4B08 **What transmitter performance parameter does a two-tone test analyze?**

A. Linearity
B. Percentage of suppression of the carrier and undesired sideband for SSB
C. Percentage of frequency modulation
D. Percentage of carrier phase shift

(A) See G4B07 [*General Class License Manual*, page 5-8]

G4B09 **When is an analog multimeter preferred to a digital multimeter?**

A. When testing logic circuits
B. When high precision is desired
C. When measuring the frequency of an oscillator
D. When adjusting circuits for maximum or minimum values

(D) See G4B07 [*General Class License Manual*, page 4-43]

G4B10 **Which of the following can be determined with a directional wattmeter?**

A. Standing wave ratio
B. Antenna front-to-back ratio
C. RF interference
D. Radio wave propagation

(A) SWR can be calculated from forward and reflected power measurements made using a directional wattmeter. SWR is then calculated using the following formula:

$$SWR = \frac{1 + \sqrt{P_R / P_F}}{1 - \sqrt{P_R / P_F}}$$

where P_F is forward power and P_R is reflected power. [*General Class License Manual*, page 4-43]

G4B11 **Which of the following must be connected to an antenna analyzer when it is being used for SWR measurements?**

A. Receiver
B. Transmitter
C. Antenna and feed line
D. All these choices are correct

(C) An antenna analyzer is the equivalent of a very low power, adjustable-frequency transmitter and SWR bridge. The antenna and feed line are connected to the analyzer and SWR measurements are made directly from the analyzer's meter or display while the analyzer frequency is adjusted. This is much more convenient than using a transmitter and wattmeter and also minimizes the potential for interfering with other signals. [*General Class License Manual*, page 4-43]

G4B12   What effect can strong signals from nearby transmitters have on an antenna analyzer?

A. Desensitization which can cause intermodulation products which interfere with impedance readings
B. Received power that interferes with SWR readings
C. Generation of harmonics which interfere with frequency readings
D. All these choices are correct

(B)   Because an analyzer's SWR bridge must be sensitive enough to work with the low-power transmitter, it is also sensitive to RF that the antenna may pick up. This is a particular problem when using the analyzer near broadcast stations with their high-powered transmitters. Symptoms might include SWR readings that change with station programming and excessively high or low SWR that does not change with frequency as expected. [*General Class License Manual*, page 4-43]

G4B13   Which of the following can be measured with an antenna analyzer?

A. Front-to-back ratio of an antenna
B. Power output from a transmitter
C. Impedance of coaxial cable
D. Gain of a directional antenna

(C)   An antenna analyzer's manual will show how to make many useful measurements such as feed line characteristic impedance, velocity of propagation, electrical length, and so on. These are very flexible test instruments. [*General Class License Manual*, page 4-43]

G4C — Interference to consumer electronics; grounding and bonding

G4C01   Which of the following might be useful in reducing RF interference to audio frequency circuits?

A. Bypass inductor
B. Bypass capacitor
C. Forward-biased diode
D. Reverse-biased diode

(B)   If radio frequency interference is entering a home audio system through external control cables or power leads, a bypass capacitor can be effective at keeping the unwanted RF signal out of the equipment. With transistor or integrated circuit audio amplifiers you may need to use RF chokes in series with the speaker leads instead of a bypass capacitor. See the *ARRL Handbook* for more information on finding and fixing RFI problems. [*General Class License Manual*, page 5-21]

G4C02 Which of the following could be a cause of interference covering a wide range of frequencies?

A. Not using a balun or line isolator to feed balanced antennas
B. Lack of rectification of the transmitter's signal in power conductors
C. Arcing at a poor electrical connection
D. Using a balun to feed an unbalanced antenna

(C) An arc, such as in motors or at the contacts of electrical equipment, is rich in harmonic energy, even though the primary current may be dc or 60 Hz ac. The resulting RF harmonics can be radiated by the power wiring as broadband noise heard by nearby receivers. Broadband noise can also be caused by intermittent or poor contacts in RF circuits in your own station. [*General Class License Manual*, page 5-21]

G4C03 What sound is heard from an audio device experiencing RF interface from a single sideband phone transmitter?

A. A steady hum whenever the transmitter is on the air
B. On-and-off humming or clicking
C. Distorted speech
D. Clearly audible speech

(C) An audio device or telephone can sometimes rectify and detect RF signals in much the same way that an AM broadcast radio does. The audio signal is then amplified resulting in interference. The amateur's voice will be heard but it will be highly distorted. [*General Class License Manual*, page 5-21]

G4C04 What sound is heard from an audio device experiencing RF interference from a CW transmitter?

A. On-and-off humming or clicking
B. A CW signal at a nearly pure audio frequency
C. A chirpy CW signal
D. Severely distorted audio

(A) See G4C03 — the amateur's CW transmission will be heard as on-and-off humming or clicking in a Morse code-like pattern. [*General Class License Manual*, page 5-21]

G4C05 **What is a possible cause of high voltages that produce RF burns?**

A. Flat braid rather than round wire has been used for the ground wire
B. Insulated wire has been used for the ground wire
C. The ground rod is resonant
D. The ground wire has high impedance on that frequency

(D) If the connection to a ground rod is long enough, it can be an odd multiple of ¼-wavelength long on one or more bands. This resonance results in the wire having a high impedance on that band, which enables high RF voltages to be present on the chassis of your equipment or microphone. The high voltage will cause an RF burn if the "hot spot" is touched when you are transmitting. RF burns are painful but rarely cause significant injury. The ARRL's Safety web page (**arrl.org/safety**) includes a great deal of useful information about station grounding and managing RF voltage and current [*General Class License Manual*, page 5-21]

G4C06 **What is a possible effect of a resonant ground connection?**

A. Overheating of ground straps
B. Corrosion of the ground rod
C. High RF voltages on the enclosures of station equipment
D. A ground loop

(C) See G4C05. [*General Class License Manual*, page 5-21]

G4C07 **Why should soldered joints not be used in lightning protection ground connections?**

A. A soldered joint will likely be destroyed by the heat of a lightning strike
B. Solder flux will prevent a low conductivity connection
C. Solder has too high a dielectric constant to provide adequate lightning protection
D. All these choices are correct

(A) Do not use solder to make the connections since solder joints would likely melt and be destroyed if hit with a lightning-sized current pulse. Use mechanical clamps, brazing, or welding to be sure the ground connection is heavy enough. [*General Class License Manual*, page 9-8]

G4C08 Which of the following would reduce RF interference caused by common-mode current on an audio cable?

A. Place a ferrite choke on the cable
B. Connect the center conductor to the shield of all cables to short circuit the RFI signal
C. Ground the center conductor of the audio cable causing the interference
D. Add an additional insulating jacket to the cable

(A) The best solution to many types of interference caused by proximity to an amateur station is to keep the RF signals from entering the equipment in the first place. If filters can be used, they are generally the most effective and least troublesome to install. The next approach is to prevent RF current from flowing by placing inductance or resistance in its path. This is done by forming the conductor carrying the RF current into an RF choke, winding it around or through a ferrite core. Ferrite beads and cores can also be placed on cables to prevent RF common-mode current from flowing on the outside of cable braids or shields. [*General Class License Manual*, page 5-21]

G4C09 How can the effects of ground loops be minimized?

A. Connect all ground conductors in series
B. Connect the AC neutral conductor to the ground wire
C. Avoid using lock washers and star washers when making ground connections
D. Bond equipment enclosures together

(D) Ground loops are created when a continuous current path (the loop) exists through a series of equipment enclosures and cables. The loop acts as a single-turn inductor that picks up voltages from magnetic fields generated by power transformers, ac wiring and other low-frequency currents. The result is a hum or buzz in audio signals or an ac signal that interferes with control or data signals. Less frequently, the loop can pick up transmitted RF and cause distortion in audio signals. Since the many interconnections in an amateur station make it impossible to avoid loops, minimize the loop's area and inductance by using short cables and bundling them together. [*General Class License Manual*, page 5-22]

G4C10 What could be a symptom caused by a ground loop in your station's audio connections?

A. You receive reports of "hum" on your station's transmitted signal
B. The SWR reading for one or more antennas is suddenly very high
C. An item of station equipment starts to draw excessive amounts of current
D. You receive reports of harmonic interference from your station

(A) See G4C09. [*General Class License Manual*, page 5-22]

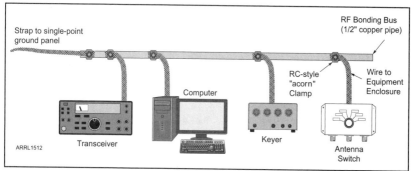

Figure G4.1 — A typical bonding bus for a station with equipment on a table or desk. By connecting equipment together using short, heavy connections, voltage differences are minimized.

G4C11   What technique helps to minimize RF "hot spots" in an amateur station?

A. Building all equipment in a metal enclosure
B. Using surge suppressor power outlets
C. Bonding all equipment enclosures together
D. Placing low-pass filters on all feed lines

(C)   The basics for RF bonding in your station are:

• Connect all metal equipment enclosures directly together or to a common RF bonding bus (see **Figure G4.1**).

• Keep all connections, straps and wires short.

• Use short, heavy conductors such as heavy wire (#12 or #14 AWG) or strap.

Where strong RF signals are present, a piece of wide flashing or screen can be placed under the equipment and connected to the RF bonding bus. [*General Class License Manual*, page 5-22]

G4C12   Why must all metal enclosures of station equipment be grounded?

A. It prevents a blown fuse in the event of an internal short circuit
B. It prevents signal overload
C. It ensures that the neutral wire is grounded
D. It ensures that hazardous voltages cannot appear on the chassis

(D)   Any equipment with an exposed metal enclosure must be grounded. This prevents hazardous voltages from appearing on the equipment chassis, creating a shock hazard. [*General Class License Manual*, page 5-22]

G4D — Speech processors; S meters; sideband operation near band edges

G4D01 What is the purpose of a speech processor in a transceiver?

A. Increase the apparent loudness of transmitted voice signals
B. Increase transmitter bass response for more natural-sounding SSB signals
C. Prevent distortion of voice signals
D. Decrease high-frequency voice output to prevent out-of-band operation

(A) A speech processor can improve signal intelligibility by raising average power without increasing peak envelope power (PEP). It does this by amplifying low-level signals more than high-level signals. As a result, the average signal level is increased. A speech processor does not increase the transmitter output PEP. See **Figure G4.2**. [*General Class License Manual*, page 5-8]

G4D02 How does a speech processor affect a single sideband phone signal?

A. It increases peak power
B. It increases average power
C. It reduces harmonic distortion
D. It reduces intermodulation distortion

(B) See G4D01. [*General Class License Manual*, page 5-7]

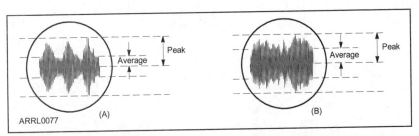

Figure G4.2 — A typical SSB voice-modulated signal might have an envelope similar to the oscilloscope display shown at A. After speech processing, the envelope pattern might look like the display at B. The average power of the processed signal has increased, but the PEP is unchanged.

G4D03   Which if the effect of an incorrectly adjusted speech processor?

A. Distorted speech
B. Excess intermodulation products
C. Excessive background noise
D. All these choices are correct

(D)   Proper adjustment of a speech processor is important to ensure your transmitted signal is not distorted and is free of spurious signals. Excessive processing causes your speech to be distorted. Processors can also amplify background noise from fans and other radios and combine them with your desired speech. Another common result of too much processing is overdriving the transmitter output stages, causing interference ("splatter") to signals on nearby frequencies. Read the owner's manual for your radio and learn to operate its speech processor. Practice on the air with a friend to insure you are adjusting the processor correctly. [*General Class License Manual*, page 5-8]

G4D04   What does an S meter measure?

A. Carrier suppression
B. Impedance
C. Received signal strength
D. Transmitter power output

(C)   An S-meter measures received signal strength in S-units. [*General Class License Manual*, page 5-16]

G4D05   How does a signal that reads 20 dB over S9 compare to one that reads S9 on a receiver, assuming a properly calibrated S meter?

A. It is 10 times less powerful
B. It is 20 times less powerful
C. It is 20 times more powerful
D. It is 100 times more powerful

(D)   An ideal S-meter operates on a logarithmic scale, indicating one S-unit of change for a four-times increase or decrease in power. (This is a 6-dB change in power.) Most actual S-meters are only calibrated to that standard in the middle of their range (if at all). Above S-9, theoretically corresponding to a 50 μV input signal, S-meters are calibrated in dB. In the example of this question, a signal 20 dB stronger than S-9 is 100 times stronger than S-9. [*General Class License Manual*, page 5-16]

G4D06 How much change in signal strength is typically represented by one S unit?

A. 6 dB
B. 12 dB
C. 15 dB
D. 18 dB

(A)   See G4D05. [*General Class License Manual*, page 5-16]

G4D07 How much must the power output of a transmitter be raised to change the S meter reading on a distant receiver from S8 to S9?

A. Approximately 1.5 times
B. Approximately 2 times
C. Approximately 4 times
D. Approximately 8 times

(C)   For an ideal S-meter, one S-unit of change corresponds to a four-times increase or decrease in power. This is a 6 dB change in power. (See also G4D05.) [*General Class License Manual*, page 5-16]

G4D08 What frequency range is occupied by a 3 kHz LSB signal when the displayed carrier frequency is set to 7.178 MHz?

A. 7.178 to 7.181 MHz
B. 7.178 to 7.184 MHz
C. 7.175 to 7.178 MHz
D. 7.1765 to 7.1795 MHz

(C)   Nearly all radios display the carrier frequency of a SSB transmission. That means your actual signal lies entirely above (USB) or below (LSB) the displayed frequency. If the sidebands occupy 3 kHz of spectrum, you'll need to stay far enough from the edge of your frequency privileges to avoid transmitting a signal outside them. For example, Generals are permitted to use up to 14.350 MHz, so the displayed carrier frequency of a 3 kHz-wide USB signal should be no less than 3 kHz from the band edge — 14.347 MHz — and the signal occupies 14.347 to 14.350 MHz. If you transmit higher than that, the sidebands begin to extend into the non-amateur frequencies above 14.350 MHz! Similarly, using 3 kHz-wide LSB on 40 meters, Generals should operate with the carrier frequency no less than 3 kHz above the band edge — 7.178 MHz — thus occupying the range of 7.175 to 7.178 MHz. See **Figure G4.3**. [*General Class License Manual*, page 5-8]

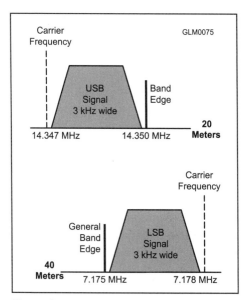

Figure G4.3 — When the sidebands of a typical 3 kHz-wide SSB signal extend from the carrier towards a band edge or a band segment edge, operate with a displayed carrier frequency no closer than 3 kHz to the edge frequency and be sure your signal is "clean."

G4D09 What frequency range is occupied by a 3 kHz USB signal with the displayed carrier frequency set to 14.347 MHz?

A. 14.347 to 14.647 MHz
B. 14.347 to 14.350 MHz
C. 14.344 to 14.347 MHz
D. 14.3455 to 14.3485 MHz

(B) See G4D08. [*General Class License Manual*, page 5-8]

G4D10 How close to the lower edge of a band's phone segment should your displayed carrier frequency be when using 3 kHz wide LSB?

A. At least 3 kHz above the edge of the segment
B. At least 3 kHz below the edge of the segment
C. At least 1 kHz below the edge of the segment
D. At least 1 kHz above the edge of the segment

(A) See G4D08. [*General Class License Manual*, page 5-8]

G4D11 How close to the upper edge of a band's phone segment should your displayed carrier frequency be when using 3 kHz wide USB?

A. At least 3 kHz above the edge of the band
B. At least 3 kHz below the edge of the band
C. At least 1 kHz above the edge of the segment
D. At least 1 kHz below the edge of the segment

(B) See G4D08. [*General Class License Manual*, page 5-8]

G4E — Mobile and Portable HF stations; alternative energy source operation

G4E01 What is the purpose of a capacitance hat on a mobile antenna?

A. To increase the power handling capacity of a whip antenna
B. To reduce radiation resistance
C. To electrically lengthen a physically short antenna
D. To lower the radiation angle

(C) A structure of rods and possibly a ring added at or near the top of the antenna is called a capacitance hat or capacity hat. It increases the capacitance of a mobile antenna and electrically lengthens it so that it can be used effectively at lower frequencies. [*General Class License Manual*, page 7-1]

G4E02 What is the purpose of a corona ball on an HF mobile antenna?

A. To narrow the operating bandwidth of the antenna
B. To increase the "Q" of the antenna
C. To reduce the chance of damage if the antenna should strike an object
D. To reduce RF voltage discharge from the tip of the antenna while transmitting

(D) The sharp tip of mobile whip can result in corona discharge from high RF voltages even at moderate power levels. By adding a smooth ball, the tendency for corona to form is reduced [*General Class License Manual*, page 7-1]

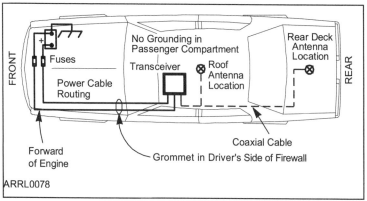

Figure G4.4 — A typical mobile transceiver's installation and wiring system.

G4E03 Which of the following direct, fused power connections would be the best for a 100 watt HF mobile installation?

A. To the battery using heavy-gauge wire
B. To the alternator or generator using heavy-gauge wire
C. To the battery using insulated heavy duty balanced transmission line
D. To the alternator or generator using insulated heavy duty balanced transmission line

(A) When you are making the power connections for your 100-watt HF radio for mobile operation, connect heavy-gauge wires directly to the battery terminals. Both leads should have fuses, placed as close to the battery as possible. See **Figure G4.4**. [*General Class License Manual*, page 5-22]

G4E04 Why should DC power for a 100-watt HF transceiver not be supplied by a vehicle's auxiliary power socket?

A. The socket is not wired with an RF-shielded power cable
B. The socket's wiring may be inadequate for the current drawn by the transceiver
C. The DC polarity of the socket is reversed from the polarity of modern HF transceivers
D. Drawing more than 50 watts from this socket could cause the engine to overheat

(B) The auxiliary socket wiring is adequate for a low-power hand-held radio but not for a full-power HF transceiver drawing 20 amps or more when transmitting. Use a direct connection to the battery. (See also G4E03.) [*General Class License Manual*, page 5-22]

G4E05 **Which of the following most limits an HF mobile installation?**

A. "Picket fencing"
B. The wire gauge of the DC power line to the transceiver
C. Efficiency of the electrically short antenna
D. FCC rules limiting mobile output power on the 75-meter band

(C) HF mobile antenna systems are the most limiting factor for effective operation of your station. Placing even an 8-foot vertical antenna on top of a small car makes a dangerously tall system. If you have a taller vehicle, this kind of antenna is almost out of the question. Some type of inductive loading to shorten the length is then required. [*General Class License Manual*, page 5-22]

G4E06 **What is one disadvantage of using a shortened mobile antenna as opposed to a full size antenna?**

A. Short antennas are more likely to cause distortion of transmitted signals
B. Q of the antenna will be very low
C. Operating bandwidth may be very limited
D. Harmonic radiation may increase

(C) Electrically short antennas present a very low impedance at their base, the usual location of the feed point. This causes the frequency range to be very narrow over which a matching network presents a 50 ohm impedance to the transmitter. [*General Class License Manual*, page 7-1]

G4E07 **Which of the following may cause receive interference to an HF transceiver installed in a vehicle?**

A. The battery charging system
B. The fuel delivery system
C. The control computers
D. All these choices are correct

(D) High-current pulses and switching from the battery charging system can easily create signals at RF which can cause interference. Similarly, the dc motors associated with electric fuel pumps are also frequent sources of interference. Digital signals internal and external to the vehicle's control computer system can radiate from the vehicle's electrical wiring and be received at RF, as well. [*General Class License Manual*, page 5-22]

G4E08 **In what configuration are the individual cells in a solar panel connected together?**

A. Series-parallel
B. Shunt
C. Bypass
D. Full-wave bridge

(A) What is most often meant by "solar power" is really photovoltaic conversion of sunlight directly to electricity. Solar panels and solar cells are made of silicon PN-junctions that are exposed to sunlight and arranged in a series-parallel configuration. [*General Class License Manual*, page 4-37]

G4E09 **What is the approximate open-circuit voltage from a fully illuminated silicon photovoltaic cell?**

A. 0.02 VDC
B. 0.5 VDC
C. 0.2 VDC
D. 1.38 VDC

(B) Each photovoltaic cell produces about 0.5 volt in full sunlight if there is no load connected to the cell. The size or surface area of the cell determines the maximum current that the cell can supply. [*General Class License Manual*, page 4-37]

G4E10 **Why should a series diode be connected between a solar panel and a storage battery that is being charged by the panel?**

A. To prevent overload by regulating the charging voltage
B. To prevent discharge of the battery through the panel during times of low or no illumination
C. To limit the current flowing from the panel to a safe value
D. To prevent damage to the battery due to excessive voltage at high illumination levels

(B) If connected directly to a battery, during periods of low or no illumination, the battery voltage will be higher than that from the panel, allowing the battery to discharge back through the panel. [*General Class License Manual*, page 4-37]

G4E11   **What precaution should be taken when connecting a solar panel to a lithium iron phosphate battery?**

A. Ground the solar panel outer metal framework
B. Ensure the battery is placed terminals-up
C. A series resistor must be in place
D. The solar panel must have a charge controller

(D)   When connecting a solar panel to a lithium iron phosphate battery (like a LiFePO4),you should use a charge controller to avoid overcharging the battery, which can be a safety concern and can also decrease the battery's usable lifespan. [*General Class License Manual*, page 4-38]

Electrical Principles

[3 Exam Questions — 3 Groups]

G5A — Reactance; inductance; capacitance; impedance; impedance transformation; resonance

G5A01   What happens when inductive and capacitive reactance are equal in a series LC circuit?
A. Resonance causes impedance to be very high
B. Impedance is equal to the geometric mean of the inductance and capacitance
C. Resonance causes impedance to be very low
D. Impedance is equal to the arithmetic mean of the inductance and capacitance

(C)   In a series LC circuit, when inductive and capacitative reactance are equal, resonance causes the impedance to be very low. [*General Class License Manual*, page 4-23]

G5A02   What is reactance?
A. Opposition to the flow of direct current caused by resistance
B. Opposition to the flow of alternating current caused by capacitance or inductance
C. Reinforcement of the flow of direct current caused by resistance
D. Reinforcement of the flow of alternating current caused by capacitance or inductance

(B)   The opposition to flow of ac current caused by inductance and capacitance is referred to as reactance. Reactance is one component of impedance, along with resistance. [*General Class License Manual*, page 4-20]

G5A03   Which of the following is opposition to the flow of alternating current in an inductor?
A. Conductance
B. Reluctance
C. Admittance
D. Reactance

(D)   The opposition to flow of current in an alternating current (ac) circuit caused by an inductor is referred to as inductive reactance. (See also G5A02.) [*General Class License Manual*, page 4-20]

G5A04   Which of the following is opposition to the flow of
alternating current in a capacitor?
  A. Conductance
  B. Reluctance
  C. Reactance
  D. Admittance

(C)   The opposition to flow of current in an alternating current (ac) circuit
caused by a capacitor is referred to as capacitive reactance. (See also G5A02.)
[*General Class License Manual*, page 4-20]

G5A05   How does an inductor react to AC?
  A. As the frequency of the applied AC increases, the reactance
     decreases
  B. As the amplitude of the applied AC increases, the reactance increases
  C. As the amplitude of the applied AC increases, the reactance
     decreases
  D. As the frequency of the applied AC increases, the reactance increases

(D)   Inductive reactance increases as the ac frequency increases. (See also
G5A03.) [*General Class License Manual*, page 4-20]

G5A06   How does a capacitor react to AC?
  A. As the frequency of the applied AC increases, the reactance
     decreases
  B. As the frequency of the applied AC increases, the reactance increases
  C. As the amplitude of the applied AC increases, the reactance increases
  D. As the amplitude of the applied AC increases, the reactance
     decreases

(A)   Capacitive reactance decreases as the ac frequency increases. (See also
G5A04.) [*General Class License Manual*, page 4-20]

G5A07   What is the term for the inverse of impedance?
  A. Conductance
  B. Susceptance
  C. Reluctance
  D. Admittance

(D)   The inverse of impedance is called admittance. [*General Class License
Manual*, page 4-23]

G5A08   What is impedance?

A. The ratio of current to voltage
B. The product of current and voltage
C. The ratio of voltage to current
D. The product of current and reactance

(C)   Impedance is a general term for the opposition to current flow in an ac circuit caused by resistance (Z), reactance (X), or any combination of the two. Impedance is symbolized by the letter Z and measured in ohms. [*General Class License Manual*, page 4-23]

G5A09   What unit is used to measure reactance?

A. Farad
B. Ohm
C. Ampere
D. Siemens

(B)   The ohm is the unit used to measure any opposition to the flow of current. In an ac circuit, this opposition is referred to as impedance which includes both reactance and resistance. (See also G5A08.) [*General Class License Manual*, page 4-20]

G5A10   Which of the following devices can be used for impedance matching at radio frequencies?

A. A transformer
B. A Pi-network
C. A length of transmission line
D. All these choices are correct

(D)   All of these can alter the ratio of voltage and current in a circuit, changing the impedance as well. Special lengths of transmission lines can be used to set up patterns of reflections in the feed line that cancel the reflections from a mismatched load, making the load impedance appear as if it was the same as that of the feed line. [*General Class License Manual*, page 4-23]

G5A11   What letter is used to represent reactance?

A. Z
B. X
C. B
D. Y

(B)   See G5A08. [*General Class License Manual*, page 4-23]

G5A12   What occurs in an LC circuit at resonance?

A. Current and voltage are equal
B. Resistance is cancelled
C. The circuit radiates all its energy in the form of radio waves
D. Inductive reactance and capacitive reactance cancel

(D)   An LC network, such as a pi-notwork, uses the exchange of stored energy between the inductor and capacitors to transform the ratio of voltage and current (impedence) at its input and output while transferring power between them. Common examples of impedance matching LC networks are the L-, T-, and Pi-networks. named for the resemblance to a letter of the arrangement of their components on a schematic. At resonance in a parallel circuit, inductive and capacitive reactances cancel. [*General Class License Manual*, page 4-23]

G5B — The decibel; current and voltage dividers; electrical power calculations; sine wave root-mean-square (RMS) values; PEP calculations

G5B01   What dB change represents a factor of two increase or decrease in power?

A. Approximately 2 dB
B. Approximately 3 dB
C. Approximately 6 dB
D. Approximately 12 dB

(B)   The decibel scale is a logarithmic scale in which a two-times increase (or decrease) in power is represented by 3 dB. The mathematical formula for the decibel scale for power is:

$$dB = 10 \times \log_{10}\left(\frac{P_2}{P_1}\right)$$

where P_1 = reference power and P_2 = power being compared to the reference value.

In this case:

$$dB = 10 \times \log_{10}\left(\frac{2}{1}\right) = 10 \times \log_{10}(2) = 10 \times 0.3 = 3\,dB$$

[*General Class License Manual*, page 4-1]

Table G5.1
Some Common Decibel Values and Power Ratio Equivalents

dB	P_2 / P_1
20	100 (10^2)
10	10 (10^1)
6	4
3	2
0	1
−3	0.5
−6	0.25
−10	0.1 (10^{-1})
−20	0.01 (10^{-2})

G5B02 **How does the total current relate to the individual currents in a circuit of parallel resistors?**

A. It equals the average of the branch currents
B. It decreases as more parallel branches are added to the circuit
C. It equals the sum of the currents through each branch
D. It is the sum of the reciprocal of each individual voltage drop

(C) In a circuit with several parallel branches, the total current flowing into the junction of the branches is equal to the sum of the current through each branch. This is Kirchoff's Current Law. See **Figure G5.1**. [*General Class License Manual*, page 4-15]

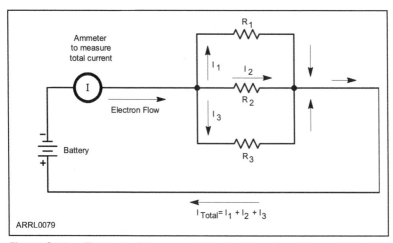

Figure G5.1 — The sum of the current flowing into a junction point (node) in a circuit must be equal to the current flowing out of the junction point (node). This principle is called Kirchhoff's Current Law, named for Gustav Kirchhoff, the German scientist who discovered it.

G5B03 How many watts of electrical power are consumed if 400 VDC is supplied to an 800-ohm load?

A. 0.5 watts
B. 200 watts
C. 400 watts
D. 3200 watts

(B) Since P = I × E and I = E/R, the power in a circuit also can be expressed as

$$P = \frac{E \times E}{R}$$

In this case:

$$P = \frac{400 \times 400}{800} = \frac{160,000}{800} = 200\,W$$

[*General Class License Manual*, page 4-1]

G5B04 How many watts of electrical power are consumed by a 12 VDC light bulb that draws 0.2 amperes?

A. 2.4 watts
B. 24 watts
C. 6 watts
D. 60 watts

(A) Use the Power Circle (**Figure G5.2**) to find the equation for calculating power. In this case, power is equal to the voltage times the current: P = I × E = 0.2 × 12 = 2.4 watts. [*General Class License Manual*, page 4-1]

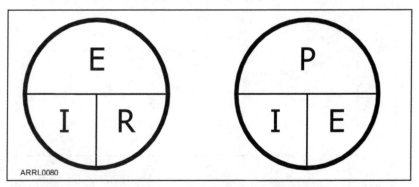

ARRL0080

Figure G5.2 — The "Ohm's Law Circle" and the "Power Circle" will help you remember the equations that include voltage, current, resistance and power. Cover the letter representing the unknown quantity to find an equation to calculate that quantity. If you cover the I in the Ohm's Law Circle, you are left with E/R. If you cover the P in the Power Circle, you are left with I × E. Combining these terms, you can write the equation to calculate power when you know the voltage and the resistance.

G5B05 **How many watts are consumed when a current of 7.0 milliamperes flows through a 1,250-ohm resistance?**

A. Approximately 61 milliwatts
B. Approximately 61 watts
C. Approximately 11 milliwatts
D. Approximately 11 watts

(A)   Use the Ohm's Law Circle and Power Circle drawings to find the equations to calculate power. Since P = I × E and E = R × I, the power in a circuit can also be expressed as P = I × I × R, so P = 0.007 × 0.007 × 1250 = 0.06125 W = 61.25 mW. Remember that 7 milliamperes is equal to 0.007 ampere, 1.25 kilohms is equal to 1250 ohms and 0.06125 watt is equal to approximately 61 milliwatts. [*General Class License Manual*, page 4-1]

G5B06 **What is the PEP produced by 200 volts peak-to-peak across a 50-ohm dummy load?**

A. 1.4 watts
B. 100 watts
C. 353.5 watts
D. 400 watts

(B)   PEP is the output power of one complete RF cycle at the peak of the signal's envelope and is equal to:

$$PEP = \frac{(\text{Peak envelope voltage} \times 0.707)^2}{R}$$

Peak envelope voltage = Peak-to-peak envelope voltage / 2, so:

$$PEP = \frac{(100 \times 0.707)^2}{50} = 100\,\text{W}$$

[*General Class License Manual*, page 4-6]

G5B07 **What value of an AC signal produces the same power dissipation in a resistor as a DC voltage of the same value?**

A. The peak-to-peak value
B. The peak value
C. The RMS value
D. The reciprocal of the RMS value

(C)   RMS, or root mean square, voltage values convert a constantly-varying ac voltage to the equivalent of a constant dc voltage. The RMS value of an ac voltage would deliver the same amount of power to a resistance as a dc voltage of the same value. [*General Class License Manual*, page 4-5]

G5B08 **What is the peak-to-peak voltage of a sine wave with an RMS voltage of 120 volts?**

A. 84.8 volts
B. 169.7 volts
C. 240.0 volts
D. 339.4 volts

(D) $V_{PK-PK} = V_{RMS} \times 1.414 \times 2 = 120 \times 1.414 \times 2 = 339.4$ V [*General Class License Manual*, page 4-5]

G5B09 **What is the RMS voltage of a sine wave with a value of 17 volts peak?**

A. 8.5 volts
B. 12 volts
C. 24 volts
D. 34 volts

(B) If you know the peak voltage, you can find the RMS value by multiplying the peak voltage by 0.707 (which is the same as dividing by the square root of 2): $17 \times 0.707 = 12$ V. See **Figure G5.3**. [*General Class License Manual*, page 4-5]

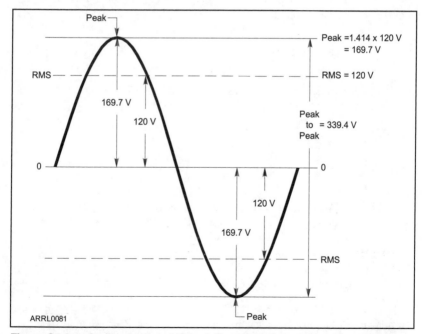

Figure G5.3 — An illustration of the relationship between ac measurements for sine wave waveforms. RMS value conversions assume that the waveform is a sine wave. Different conversion values are required for other waveform shapes, such as square or triangle waves.

G5B10 What percentage of power loss is equivalent to a loss of 1 dB?

    A. 10.9 percent
    B. 12.2 percent
    C. 20.6 percent
    D. 25.9 percent

(C)   See also G5B01. In this question we are told that the transmission line to an antenna results in a signal loss of 1 dB. We can use the decibel equation to calculate the power that reaches the antenna through this feed line, and from that we can calculate the power lost in the feed line. If we assume a transmitter power of 100 W, then the answer will be the percentage of the original power that is lost in the feed line. First, we will solve the decibel equation for P_2, the power that reaches the antenna.

$$dB = 10 \times \log_{10}\left(\frac{P_2}{P_1}\right)$$

$$\frac{dB}{10} = \log_{10}\left(\frac{P_2}{P_1}\right)$$

$$\log_{10}^{-1}\left(\frac{dB}{10}\right) = \left(\frac{P_2}{P_1}\right)$$

$$P_1 \log_{10}^{-1}\left(\frac{dB}{10}\right) = P_2$$

Note: The notation that shows the logarithm raised to the negative 1 power means the antilog, or inverse logarithm. On some scientific calculators this button is also labeled 10^x, which means "raise 10 to the power of this value." The decibel value is given as a loss of 1 dB, so we will write that as −1 dB.

$$100\,W \times \log_{10}^{-1}\left(\frac{-1\,dB}{10}\right) = 100\,W \times 0.794 = 79.4\,W$$

If 79.4 W is the power actually reaching the antenna, then we can calculate the lost power by subtracting this value from the original power: 100 W − 79.4 W = 20.6 W.

Because we used 100 W as the reference power, this value is the percentage of the original power that is lost in our feed line, when it has a loss of 1 dB. The percentage of the power lost in this feed line is 20.6%.

[*General Class License Manual*, page 4-1]

G5B11   What is the ratio of PEP to average power for an unmodulated carrier?

A. 0.707
B. 1.00
C. 1.414
D. 2.00

(B)   The ratio is 1.0 because for an unmodulated carrier all RF cycles have the same voltage, meaning that the envelope's average and peak values are the same. [*General Class License Manual*, page 4-5]

G5B12   What is the RMS voltage across a 50-ohm dummy load dissipating 1200 watts?

A. 173 volts
B. 245 volts
C. 346 volts
D. 692 volts

(B)   The voltage is 245 V because $P = E^2 / R$, so $E = \sqrt{1200 \times 50}$. This is the RMS voltage across the 50 ohm load. [*General Class License Manual*, page 4-5]

G5B13   What is the output PEP of an unmodulated carrier if the average power is 1060 watts?

A. 530 watts
B. 1060 watts
C. 1500 watts
D. 2120 watts

(B)   The PEP and average power of an unmodulated carrier are the same. (See also G5B11.) [*General Class License Manual*, page 4-6]

G5B14   What is the output PEP of 500 volts peak-to-peak across a 50-ohm load?

A. 8.75 watts
B. 625 watts
C. 2500 watts
D. 5000 watts

(B) $PEP = (E_{RMS})^2 / R = (250 \times 0.707)^2 / 50 = 625$ W [*General Class License Manual*, page 4-6]

G5C — Resistors, capacitors, and inductors in series and parallel; transformers

G5C01   What causes a voltage to appear across the secondary winding of a transformer when an AC voltage source is connected across its primary winding?

A. Capacitive coupling
B. Displacement current coupling
C. Mutual inductance
D. Mutual capacitance

(C)   A transformer consists of two coils (windings) sharing a common core so that the flux from current flowing in one winding is shared by both windings (see **Figure G5.4**). When current flows through the primary winding it creates a magnetic field in the core. That magnetic field changes polarity and strength as the primary ac voltage changes. The changing magnetic field in the common core is shared by the secondary winding, inducing a voltage across the turns of the secondary winding and creating a current in the secondary circuit. The core material might be layers of steel, a powdered iron mixture, some other magnetic material, or even air. The coupling between the primary and secondary windings is called mutual inductance. [*General Class License Manual*, page 4-14]

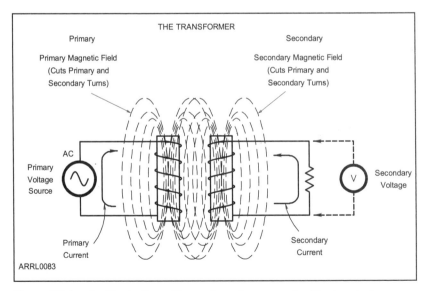

Figure G5.4 — An illustration of how a transformer works. The input of a transformer is called the primary winding, and the output is called the secondary winding. In this drawing, separate primary and secondary cores are shown to illustrate how the windings share magnetic flux. In most transformers, both windings are wound on a common core for more complete sharing of flux.

G5C02 **What is the output voltage if an input signal is applied to the secondary winding of a 4:1 voltage step-down transformer instead of the primary winding?**

A. The input voltage is multiplied by 4
B. The input voltage is divided by 4
C. Additional resistance must be added in series with the primary to prevent overload
D. Additional resistance must be added in parallel with the secondary to prevent overload

(A) The output voltage from the transformer depends on the turns ratio as described in the explanation for question G5C06. If the roles of the primary and secondary windings in transformer with an output voltage less than the input voltage by a factor of 4:1 (step-down) are reversed then the output voltage will be four times higher (step-up). [*General Class License Manual*, page 4-14]

G5C03 **What is the total resistance of a 10-, a 20-, and a 50-ohm resistor connected in parallel?**

A. 5.9 ohms
B. 0.17 ohms
C. 17 ohms
D. 80 ohms

(A) To calculate the total resistance of resistors in parallel take the reciprocal of the sum of the reistor's reciprocal values, as follows: [*General Class License Manual*, page 4-15]

$$R_{EQU} = \cfrac{1}{\cfrac{1}{10} + \cfrac{1}{20} + \cfrac{1}{50}} = 5.9\Omega$$

G5C04 **What is the approximate total resistance of a 100- and a 200-ohm resistor in parallel?**

A. 300 ohms
B. 150 ohms
C. 75 ohms
D. 67 ohms

(D) To calculate the total resistance of resistors in parallel take the reciprocal of the sum of the resistor's reciprocal values as follows:

$$R_{EQU} = \frac{100 \times 200}{100 + 200} = \frac{20,000}{300} = 66.67\Omega$$

[*General Class License Manual*, page 4-16]

G5C05 **Why is the primary winding wire of a voltage step-up transformer usually a larger size than that of the secondary winding?**

A. To improve the coupling between the primary and secondary
B. To accommodate the higher current of the primary
C. To prevent parasitic oscillations due to resistive losses in the primary
D. To ensure that the volume of the primary winding is equal to the volume of the secondary winding

(B) Transformers can change power from one combination of ac voltage and current to another by using windings with different numbers of turns. This transformation occurs because all windings share the same magnetic field by virtue of being wound on the same core. If the energy in all windings is the same but the windings have different numbers of turns, then the current in each winding must change so that the total power into and out of the transformer is the same, regardless of what load is attached to the secondary windings. A significant change between primary and secondary voltage usually requires a change in the size of wire between windings. For example, in a step-up transformer, the primary winding carries higher current and is wound with larger-diameter wire than the secondary. [*General Class License Manual*, page 4-14]

G5C06 **What is the voltage output of a transformer with a 500-turn primary and a 1500-turn secondary when 120 VAC is applied to the primary?**

A. 360 volts
B. 120 volts
C. 40 volts
D. 25.5 volts

(A) The voltage in the secondary winding of a transformer is equal to the voltage in the primary winding times the turns ratio of windings in the secondary to the primary.

$$E_S = E_P \times \text{Turns ratio} = E_P \times \frac{N_S}{N_P}$$

Since the amount of power going in and out of the transformer is the same, if voltage goes up, current must go down by the same amount:

$$I_S = I_P \times \frac{1}{\text{Turns ratio}} = I_P \times \frac{N_P}{N_S}$$

If the 500-turn primary is connected to 120 volts ac, the voltage across a 1,500-turn secondary winding in the transformer is 360 volts:

$$E_S = 120 \times \frac{1500}{500} = 360 \text{ V ac}$$

[*General Class License Manual*, page 4-14]

G5C07 **What transformer turns ratio matches an antenna's 600-ohm feed point impedance to a 50-ohm coaxial cable?**

A. 3.5 to 1
B. 12 to 1
C. 24 to 1
D. 144 to 1

(A) See G5C06. Because the transformer changes the ratio of both voltage and current between the primary and secondary, the ratio of primary and secondary impedances are controlled by the square of the turns ratio:

$$Z_{PRI} = Z_{SEC} \left(\frac{N_P}{N_S} \right)^2 \text{ and } \frac{N_P}{N_S} = \sqrt{\frac{Z_{PRI}}{Z_{SEC}}}$$

To calculate the required turns ratio:

$$\text{Turns ratio} = \frac{N_P}{N_S} = \sqrt{\frac{Z_P}{Z_S}} = \sqrt{\frac{600}{500}} = \sqrt{12} = 3.46$$

Note that the impedance to be changed (in this case 600 Ω) can be connected to the primary or secondary but turns ratios are always stated with the larger number first. In this example, it is stated as 3.46:1 not 1:3.46 (which rounds to 3.5:1). [*General Class License Manual*, page 4-23]

G5C08 **What is the equivalent capacitance of two 5.0-nanofarad capacitors and one 750-picofarad capacitor connected in parallel?**

A. 576.9 nanofarads
B. 1,733 picofarads
C. 3,583 picofarads
D. 10.750 nanofarads

(D) To calculate the total capacitance of capacitors in parallel add the values of the capacitors together,

C = C1 + C2 + C3 + …

In this case:

C = 5.0 nF + 5.0 nF + 750 pF = 5,000 pF + 5,000 pF + 750 pF = 10,750 pF

[*General Class License Manual*, page 4-16]

G5C09   **What is the capacitance of three 100-microfarad capacitors connected in series?**

A. 0.33 microfarads
B. 3.0 microfarads
C. 33.3 microfarads
D. 300 microfarads

(C)   For N capacitors with an equal common value in series, the resulting capacitance equals the common capacitor value divided by the number of capacitors,

C = Common value / N

C = 100 µF / 3 = 33.3 µF

[*General Class License Manual*, page 4-16]

G5C10   **What is the inductance of three 10-millihenry inductors connected in parallel?**

A. 0.30 henries
B. 3.3 henries
C. 3.3 millihenries
D. 30 millihenries

(C)   For N inductors with an equal common value in parallel, the resulting inductance equals the common inductor value divided by the number of inductors,

L = Common value / N

L = 10 mH / 3 = 3.3 mH

[*General Class License Manual*, page 4-16]

G5C11   **What is the inductance of a circuit with a 20-millihenry inductor connected in series with a 50-millihenry inductor?**

A. 7 millihenries
B. 14.3 millihenries
C. 70 millihenries
D. 1,000 millihenries

(C)   To calculate the total inductance in series and add the values of the inductors together,

L = L1 + L2 + L3 +...

L = 20 mH + 50 mH = 70 mH

[*General Class License Manual*, page 4-16]

G5C12 What is the capacitance of a 20-microfarad capacitor connected in series with a 50-microfarad capacitor?

A. 0.07 microfarads
B. 14.3 microfarads
C. 70 microfarads
D. 1000 microfarads

(B) To calculate the total capacitance of capacitors in series take the reciprocal of the sum of the capacitor's reciprocal values as follows:

$$C = \frac{1}{\dfrac{1}{C_1} + \dfrac{1}{C_2} + \cdots + \dfrac{1}{C_N}}$$

In the case of two capacitors in series, the equation simplifies to:

$$C = \frac{C_1 \times C_2}{C_1 + C_2} = \frac{20 \times 50}{20 + 50} = \frac{1,000}{70}$$

[*General Class License Manual*, page 4-16]

G5C13 Which of the following components should be added to a capacitor to increase the capacitance?

A. An inductor in series
B. An inductor in parallel
C. A capacitor in parallel
D. A capacitor in series

(C) Add additional capacitors in parallel to increase the total capacitance. [*General Class License Manual*, page 4-16]

G5C14 Which of the following components should be added to an inductor to increase the inductance?

A. A capacitor in series
B. A capacitor in parallel
C. An inductor in parallel
D. An inductor in series

(D) Add additional inductors in series to increase the total inductance. [*General Class License Manual*, page 4-16]

Circuit Components

[2 Exam Questions — 2 Groups]

G6A — Resistors; capacitors; inductors; rectifiers; solid-state diodes and transistors; vacuum tubes; batteries

G6A01 What is the minimum allowable discharge voltage for maximum life of a standard 12-volt lead-acid battery?
- A. 6 volts
- B. 8.5 volts
- C. 10.5 volts
- D. 12 volts

(C) Standard 12-volt lead-acid batteries are composed of six 2-volt cells connected in series. Each cell should not be discharged below 1.75 volts to avoid causing irreversible chemical changes that damage the cell. Thus, the minimum voltage for a standard 12-volt battery is 6 × 1.75 = 10.5 volts. [General Class License Manual, page 4-38]

G6A02 What is an advantage batteries with low internal resistance?
- A. Long life
- B. High discharge current
- C. High voltage
- D. Rapid recharge

(B) Nickel-cadmium (NiCd) batteries can supply large quantities of current very quickly. This makes them useful in portable power tools and radio transceivers. [*General Class License Manual*, page 4-38]

G6A03 What is the approximate forward threshold voltage of a germanium diode?
- A. 0.1 volt
- B. 0.3 volts
- C. 0.7 volts
- D. 1.0 volts

(B) The junction threshold voltage is the voltage at which a diode begins to conduct significant current across its PN junction. The amount of voltage depends on the material from which the diode is constructed. The junction threshold voltage of silicon diodes is approximately 0.7 V and for germanium diodes approximately 0.3 V. [*General Class License Manual*, page 4-25]

G6A04   **Which of the following is characteristic of an electrolytic capacitor?**

A. Tight tolerance
B. Much less leakage than any other type
C. High capacitance for a given volume
D. Inexpensive RF capacitor

(C)   Electrolytic capacitors are designed to provide large values of capacitance for energy storage and ac voltage filtering. Their construction, shown in Figure G6.1, provides relatively high capacitance in a small volume at low cost. The tradeoff is that dc voltage applied to them must always be of the same polarity, current leaks through them in relatively high amounts, and the manufacturing technique used to make them leads to rather wide variations in capacitance. [*General Class License Manual*, page 4-13]

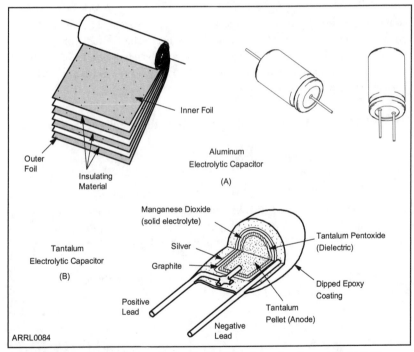

Figure G6.1 — Part A shows the construction of an aluminum electrolytic capacitor. Part B shows the construction of a tantalum electrolytic capacitor.

G6A05 **What is the approximate forward threshold voltage of a silicon junction diode?**

A. 0.1 volt
B. 0.3 volts
C. 0.7 volts
D. 1.0 volts

(C)   See G6A03 [*General Class License Manual*, page 4-25]

G6A06 **Why should wire-wound resistors not be used in RF circuits?**

A. The resistor's tolerance value would not be adequate
B. The resistor's inductance could make circuit performance unpredictable
C. The resistor could overheat
D. The resistor's internal capacitance would detune the circuit

(B)   Wire-wound resistors are made exactly as their name implies: A length of wire made from a metallic alloy with high resistance is wound around a ceramic form to reduce the overall length of the resistor. The resistor is then coated with a ceramic or other insulating material to protect the wire. If this construction method sounds like an inductor to you, you are absolutely correct! It is not a good idea to use wire-wound resistors in any RF circuits or anywhere you don't want some extra amount of inductance to be included in the circuit. The extra inductance will detune any resonant circuit to which it is connected or add unwanted inductive reactance to signal paths. [*General Class License Manual*, page 4-20]

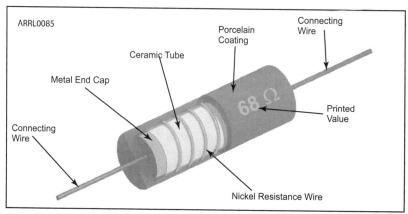

Figure G6.2 — This drawing shows the construction of a simple wire-wound resistor.

G6A07 **What are the operating points for a bipolar transistor used as a switch?**

A. Saturation and cutoff
B. The active region (between cutoff and saturation)
C. Peak and valley current points
D. Enhancement and depletion modes

(A) When a bipolar transistor is used as a switch in a logic circuit it is important that the switch either be "all the way on" or "all the way off." This is achieved by operating the transistor either in its saturation region to turn the switch on, or in its cut-off region to turn the switch off. [*General Class License Manual*, page 4-25]

G6A08 **Which of the following is characteristic of low voltage ceramic capacitors?**

A. Tight tolerance
B. High stability
C. High capacitance for given volume
D. Comparatively low cost

(D) There are many uses of capacitors in radio circuits. Each requires different characteristics that are satisfied by the various styles of capacitor construction. Here are some examples of common capacitor types and their uses:
• Ceramic — RF filtering and bypassing at high frequencies, comparatively low cost
• Plastic film — circuits operating at audio and lower radio frequencies
• Silvered-mica — highly stable, low-loss, used in RF circuits
• Electrolytic and tantalum —power supply filter circuits
• Air and vacuum dielectric — transmitting and RF circuits

G6A09 **Which of the following describes MOSFET construction?**

A. The gate is formed by a back-biased junction
B. The gate is separated from the channel by a thin insulating layer
C. The source is separated from the drain by a thin insulating layer
D. The source is formed by depositing metal on silicon

(B) A MOSFET (Metal Oxide Semiconductor Field Effect Transistor) is similar to a JFET (Junction Field Effect Transistor), but instead of the gate electrode being in direct contact with the channel between drain and source, it is insulated by a thin insulating layer of oxide. The gate voltage still controls electron flow between the drain and source, but very little current flows in the gate circuit. [*General Class License Manual*, page 4-25]

G6A10 **Which element of a vacuum tube regulates the flow of electrons between cathode and plate?**

A. Control grid
B. Suppressor grid
C. Screen grid
D. Trigger electrode

(A) The control grid is closest to the cathode, the element of the tube that generates the electrons. By varying the control grid voltage with respect to the cathode voltage, electron flow between cathode and plate can be controlled. [*General Class License Manual*, page 4-27]

G6A11 **What happens when an inductor is operated above its self-resonant frequency?**

A. Its reactance increases
B. Harmonics are generated
C. It becomes capacitive
D. Catastrophic failure is likely

(C) Resonance can also occur when a component's expected reactance is equal to the reactance of its parasitic reactance. This is called self-resonance. The result is a component that appears to be a short- or open-circuit at the self-resonant frequency. Above the self-resonant frequency, the component's reactance switches type, making an inductor capacitive and a capacitor inductive. [*General Class License Manual*, page 4-23]

G6A12 **What is the primary purpose of a screen grid in a vacuum tube?**

A. To reduce grid-to-plate capacitance
B. To increase efficiency
C. To increase the control grid resistance
D. To decrease plate resistance

(A) The screen grid is placed between the plate and control grid and kept at a constant voltage. This isolates the control grid from the plate and reduces the capacitance between them. [*General Class License Manual*, page 4-27]

G6B — Analog and digital integrated circuits (ICs); microprocessors; memory; I/O devices; microwave ICs (MMICs); display devices; connectors; ferrite cores

G6B01 What determines the performance of a ferrite core at different frequencies?

A. Its conductivity
B. Its thickness
C. The composition, or "mix," of materials used
D. The ratio of outer diameter to inner diameter

(C) Toroids may be wound on ferrite or powdered iron cores. (Ferrite is a ceramic containing iron compounds.) These cores make it possible to obtain large values of inductance in a relatively small package compared to using an air core. The combination of materials (or mix) used to make the core is selected so the inductor performs best over a specific range of frequencies. [*General Class License Manual*, page 4-11]

G6B02 What is meant by the term MMIC?

A. Multi-Mode Integrated Circuit
B. Monolithic Microwave Integrated Circuit
C. Metal Monolayer Integrated Circuit
D. Mode Modulated Integrated Circuit

(B) An MMIC is a special type of analog IC containing circuits to perform RF operations such as amplification, modulation and demodulation, and mixing at HF through microwave frequencies. Some MMICs combine several functions, acting as an entire receiver front end, for example. The MMIC is what enables communications engineers to construct low-cost, hand-held mobile phones and GPS receivers, among other sophisticated examples of wireless technology. [*General Class License Manual*, page 4-29]

G6B03 Which of the following is an advantage of CMOS integrated circuits compared to TTL integrated circuits?

A. Low power consumption
B. High power handling capability
C. Better suited for RF amplification
D. Better suited for power supply regulation

(A) Although you may find transistor-transistor logic (TTL) logic devices in some equipment, the most popular logic family in use today is the complementary metal-oxide semiconductor (CMOS) logic family because of its high speed and low power consumption. [*General Class License Manual*, page 4-29]

G6B04   What is a typical upper frequency limit for low SWR operation of 50-ohm BNC connectors?

A. 50 MHz
B. 500 MHz
C. 4 GHz
D. 40 GHz

(C)   For low power, BNC connectors are often used. BNC connectors are the standard for laboratory equipment, as well, and they are often used for dc and audio connections. BNC connectors are common on handheld radios for antenna connections. The typical upper frequency limit for low SWR operation is 4 GHz. [*General Class License Manual*, page 4-39]

G6B05   What is an advantage of using a ferrite core toroidal inductor?

A. Large values of inductance may be obtained
B. The magnetic properties of the core may be optimized for a specific range of frequencies
C. Most of the magnetic field is contained in the core
D. All these choices are correct

(D)   For a *toroidal winding* the ring-shaped core contains nearly all of the inductor's magnetic field. Since very little of the field extends outside of the core, toroidal inductors (or "toroids") can be placed next to each other in nearly any orientation with minimal mutual inductance. This property makes them ideal for use in RF circuits, where you do not want interaction between nearby inductors.

Toroids may be wound on ferrite or powdered iron cores. (Ferrite is a ceramic containing iron, zinc, and manganese compounds.) These cores make it possible to obtain largevalues of inductance in a relatively small package compared to using an air core. The combination of materials (or "mix") used to make the core is selected so the inductor performs best over a specific range of frequencies. [*General Class License Manual*, page 4-11]

G6B06   What kind of device is an integrated circuit operational amplifier?

A. Digital
B. MMIC
C. Programmable Logic
D. Analog

(D)   An operational amplifier, or op amp, is an analog circuit, operating over a continuous range of voltage and current. [*General Class License Manual*, page 4-29]

G6B07 **Which of the following describes a type N connector?**

A. A moisture-resistant RF connector useful to 10 GHz
B. A small bayonet connector used for data circuits
C. A low noise figure VHF connector
D. A nickel plated version of the PL-259

(A) Type N connectors are connectors for coaxial cable used at HF, VHF, UHF and microwave frequencies up to 10 GHz. The type N connector shell is threaded like a PL-259, but the special design of the connector body presents the same 50-Ω impedance as coaxial cable so no signal energy is reflected at the junction of connector and feed line. Type N connectors also have special gaskets built-in so that they are waterproof without requiring additional coatings. [*General Class License Manual*, page 4-39]

G6B08 **How is an LED biased when emitting light?**

A. In the tunnel-effect region
B. At the Zener voltage
C. Reverse biased
D. Forward biased

(D) A forward biased LED emits light when current flows through the PN-junction of the diode. Photons are given off when the electrons from the N-type material combine with the holes in the P-type material. [*General Class License Manual*, page 4-32]

G6B09 **How does a liquid crystal display compare to an LED display?**

A. Higher contrast in high ambient lighting
B. Wider dynamic range
C. Higher power consumption
D. Shorter lifetime

(A) A liquid crystal display (LCD) works by blocking the transmission of light through an otherwise transparent layer of liquid crystals. Transparent electrodes are printed on the glass layers on either side of the liquid crystals to form the pattern of the digits, characters, and symbols. When voltage of the right polarity is applied between the electrodes, the liquid crystals twist into a pattern that blocks light. This is why an LCD requires ambient light to reflect off the back of the display or an active source of light behind the liquid crystals (backlighting) in order to see the desired pattern. [*General Class License Manual*, page 4-32]

G6B10 How does a ferrite bead or core reduce common-mode RF current on the shield of a coaxial cable?

A. By creating an impedance in the current's path
B. It converts common-mode current to differential mode
C. By creating an out-of-phase current to cancel the common-mode current
D. Ferrites expel magnetic fields

(A) A common approach to cure RFI is to block RF current flow by placing an impedance in its path. This is done by forming the conductor carrying the RF current into an RF choke by winding it around or through a ferrite core. [*General Class License Manual*, page 5-22]

G6B11 What is an SMA connector?

A. A type-S to type-M adaptor
B. A small threaded connector suitable for signals up to several GHz
C. A connector designed for serial multiple access signals
D. A type of push-on connector intended for high-voltage applications

(B) SMA connectors are small threaded connectors designed for miniature coaxial cable and are rated for use up to 18 GHz. Handheld transceivers often use SMA connectors for attaching antennas. [*General Class License Manual*, page 4-39]

G6B12 Which of these connector types is commonly used for low frequency or dc signal connections to a transceiver?

A. PL-259
B. BNC
C. RCA Phono
D. Type N

(C) The RCA phono connector is the most common audio signal connector for consumer electronics and a great deal of amateur equipment. The connector's name derives from its early use by the RCA Company for audio connectors and its subsequent popularity for the connection of phonographs to amplifiers and receivers. [*General Class License Manual*, page 4-39]

Practical Circuits

[3 Exam Questions — 3 Groups]

G7A — Power supplies; schematic symbols

G7A01 What is the function of a power supply bleeder resistor?
A. It acts as a fuse for excess voltage
B. It discharges the filter capacitors when power is removed
C. It removes shock hazards from the induction coils
D. It eliminates ground loop current

(B) After power is turned off, the power supply filter capacitor in **Figure G7.1** cannot discharge back through the rectifier circuit, so it could remain charged for a long time. The bleeder resistor slowly discharges the capacitor, minimizing the risk of electrical shock if the supply enclosure is opened, exposing the capacitor terminals. [*General Class License Manual*, page 4-33]

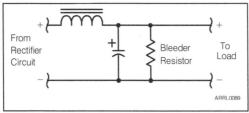

Figure G7.1 — A bleeder resistor is a safety feature that discharges a power supply filter capacitor when the supply is turned off.

G7A02 **Which of the following components are used in a power supply filter network?**

A. Diodes
B. Transformers and transducers
C. Capacitors and inductors
D. All these choices are correct

(C) A power supply filter network consists of capacitors and sometimes inductors. It is used to smooth out the pulses of voltage and current from the rectifier. Capacitors oppose changes in voltage while the inductors oppose changes in current. The combination results in a constant dc output voltage from the supply. Most power supply filters consist solely of capacitors. Inductors are generally added in high-voltage, low-current supplies. See **Figure G7.2**. [*General Class License Manual*, page 4-33]

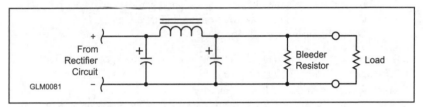

Figure G7.2 — A capacitor-input power supply filter circuit. A choke inductor and second capacitor are sometimes used in high voltage (HV) supplies for RF power amplifiers.

G7A03 **Which type of rectifier circuit uses two diodes and a center-tapped transformer?**

A. Full-wave
B. Full-wave bridge
C. Half-wave
D. Synchronous

(A) The full-wave rectifier shown in **Figure G7.3B** is really two half-wave rectifiers operating on alternate half-cycles. This rectifier requires that the transformer output winding be center-tapped to provide a return path for current that flows in the load. [*General Class License Manual*, page 4-33]

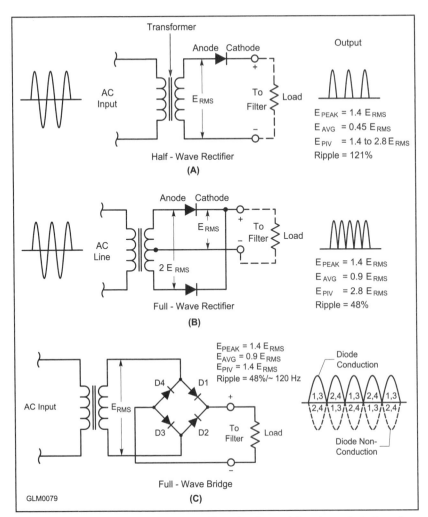

Figure G7.3 — Three fundamental rectifier circuits and the characteristics of their output voltage. (A) Half-wave. (B) Full-wave center-tapped. (C) Full-wave bridge. The half-wave rectifier circuit converts only one-half of the input waveform cycle (180°) while the full-wave circuits convert the entire cycle (360°). In most power supplies, a capacitor is connected across the output of the rectifier and will charge to a voltage of E_{PEAK}, the normal peak output of the supply.

G7A04   **What is characteristic of a half-wave rectifier in a power supply?**

A. Only one diode is required
B. The ripple frequency is twice that of a full-wave rectifier
C. More current can be drawn from the half-wave rectifier
D. The output voltage is two times the peak input voltage

(A)   The half-wave rectifier shown in Figure G7.3A uses only one diode that permits current flow during one-half of the input ac waveform (180°) from the transformer. [*General Class License Manual*, page 4-33]

G7A05   **What portion of the AC cycle is converted to DC by a half-wave rectifier?**

A. 90 degrees
B. 180 degrees
C. 270 degrees
D. 360 degrees

(B)   Since there are 360 degrees in a full cycle of ac, a half-wave rectifier converts 180 degrees of the ac input waveform to dc. [*General Class License Manual*, page 4-33]

G7A06   **What portion of the AC cycle is converted to DC by a full-wave rectifier?**

A. 90 degrees
B. 180 degrees
C. 270 degrees
D. 360 degrees

(D)   Since there are 360 degrees in a full cycle of ac, a full-wave rectifier converts 360 degrees of the ac input waveform to dc. [*General Class License Manual*, page 4-33]

G7A07 **What is the output waveform of an unfiltered full-wave rectifier connected to a resistive load?**

A. A series of DC pulses at twice the frequency of the AC input
B. A series of DC pulses at the same frequency as the AC input
C. A sine wave at half the frequency of the AC input
D. A steady DC voltage

(A) A full-wave rectifier changes alternating current with positive and negative half cycles into a fluctuating current with all positive pulses. Since the current has not been filtered, it is a series of pulses at twice the frequency of the ac input. [*General Class License Manual*, page 4-33]

G7A08 **Which of the following is characteristic of a switchmode power supply as compared to a linear power supply?**

A. Faster switching time makes higher output voltage possible
B. Fewer circuit components are required
C. High-frequency operation allows the use of smaller components
D. Inherently more stable

(C) Switchmode power supplies operate by converting ac to dc at a high frequency: 50 kHz or more is common. This allows the use of small, lightweight transformers. While the transformer in a linear power supply capable of supplying 20 amperes might weigh 15 or 20 pounds, the transformer for a switchmode power supply with a similar current rating might weigh 1 or 2 pounds! Switchmode power supplies have more complex circuits than linear supplies and generally require more components than a simple linear supply. [*General Class License Manual*, page 4-33]

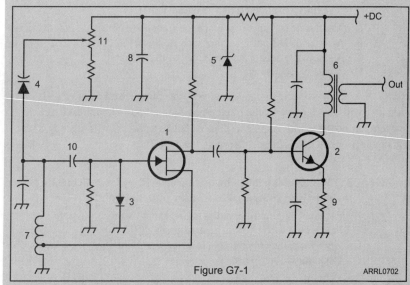

Figure G7-1   ARRL0702

Question Pool Figure G7-1 — This schematic is used in General class exam for questions G7A09 to G7A13.

G7A09   Which symbol in figure G7-1 represents a field effect transistor?

A. Symbol 2
B. Symbol 5
C. Symbol 1
D. Symbol 4

(C)   [*General Class License Manual*, page 4-8]

G7A10 Which symbol in figure G7-1 represents a Zener diode?

A. Symbol 4
B. Symbol 1
C. Symbol 11
D. Symbol 5

(D) [*General Class License Manual*, page 4-8]

G7A11 Which symbol in figure G7-1 represents an NPN junction transistor?

A. Symbol 1
B. Symbol 2
C. Symbol 7
D. Symbol 11

(B) [*General Class License Manual*, page 4-8]

G7A12 Which symbol in Figure G7-1 represents a solid core transformer?

A. Symbol 4
B. Symbol 7
C. Symbol 6
D. Symbol 1

(C) [*General Class License Manual*, page 4-8]

G7A13 Which symbol in Figure G7-1 represents a tapped inductor?

A. Symbol 7
B. Symbol 11
C. Symbol 6
D. Symbol 1

(A) [*General Class License Manual*, page 4-8]

G7B — Digital circuits; amplifiers and oscillators

G7B01   What is the purpose of neutralizing an amplifier?
- A. To limit the modulation index
- B. To eliminate self-oscillations
- C. To cut off the final amplifier during standby periods
- D. To keep the carrier on frequency

(B)   Neutralization of a power amplifier is a technique that minimizes or cancels the effects of positive feedback. Positive feedback occurs when the output signal is fed back to the input in phase with the input signal, creating an oscillator. This self-oscillation creates powerful spurious signals that cause interference. Self-oscillations can also be sufficiently powerful to damage the amplifier. Neutralization consists of feeding a portion of the amplifier output back to the input, 180 degrees out of phase with the input. This is called negative feedback. Neutralization eliminates self-oscillation by canceling the positive feedback. See **Figure G7.4**. [*General Class License Manual*, page 5-14]

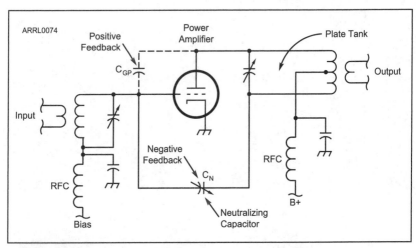

Figure G7.4 — The schematic circuit for a vacuum-tube RF power amplifier shows both the source of positive feedback that can create self-oscillation and negative feedback that cancels or neutralizes the positive feedback. Positive feedback is created by the capacitance from the plate to the grid, shows as C_{GP} on the schematic. The amount of capacitance is small, so the frequency of self-oscillation is usually at VHF or in the upper HF range. Capacitor C_N is connected to a point in the output circuit at which the signal has the opposite phase, so the feedback to the grid acts as negative feedback by providing an equal-and-opposite feedback signal to that from C_{GP}.

G7B02 **Which of these classes of amplifiers has the highest efficiency?**

A. Class A
B. Class B
C. Class AB
D. Class C

(D) Class C amplifiers act a lot like switches — they turn on for a fraction of the input signal's cycle and stay off the rest of the time. While these amplifiers are not linear at all and require filters to reduce the harmonics in their output, they are quite efficient. [*General Class License Manual*, page 5-14]

G7B03 **Which of the following describes the function of a two-input AND gate?**

A. Output is high when either or both inputs are low
B. Output is high only when both inputs are high
C. Output is low when either or both inputs are high
D. Output is low only when both inputs are high

(B) In positive-logic circuits, a high voltage represents a "true" or "1" and a low voltage represents "false" or "0". If both inputs to a positive-logic AND gate are true or "1", represented by a high input voltage, the AND function output is also "1", otherwise the output is "0", represented by a low voltage. See **Figure G7.5A**. [*General Class License Manual*, page 5-14]

G7B04 **In a Class A amplifier, what percentage of the time does the amplifying device conduct?**

A. 100%
B. More than 50% but less than 100%
C. 50%
D. Less than 50%

(A) Class A amplifiers are the most linear (lowest signal distortion) of all classes and also the least efficient. Because Class A amplifiers pass the entire sinusoidal input cycle, they conduct 100% of the time. (See also G7B03.) [*General Class License Manual*, page 5-14]

G7B05 **How many states does a 3-bit binary counter have?**

A. 3
B. 6
C. 8
D. 16

(C) There are 8 states because the number of states in a binary counter is 2^N, where N is the number of bits in the counter. A 2-bit counter has $2^2 = 4$ states, a 3-bit counter $2^3 = 8$ states, a 4-bit counter $2^4 = 16$ states, and so forth. [*General Class License Manual*, page 4-29]

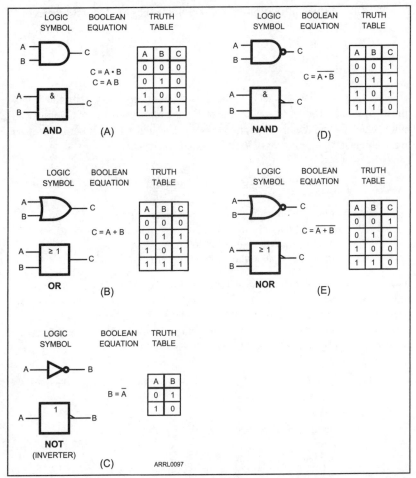

Figure G7.5 — Schematic symbols for the basic digital logic functions with the logic equations and truth tables that describe their operation. The two-input AND gate is shown at A and a two-input NOR gate at E.

G7B06 **What is a shift register?**

A. A clocked array of circuits that passes data in steps along the array
B. An array of operational amplifiers used for tri-state arithmetic operations
C. A digital mixer
D. An analog mixer

(A) A shift register consists of a sequence of flip-flop circuits with each output connected to the input of the next stage. All flip-flops share a common clock input signal. With each pulse of the clock signal, the state of the input signal (0 or 1) to the shift register is transferred to the output of the first flip-flop and each subsequent flip-flop's output is passed to the next flip-flop's input, an operation called "shifting." [*General Class License Manual*, page 4-29]

G7B07 **Which of the following are basic components of a sine wave oscillator?**

A. An amplifier and a divider
B. A frequency multiplier and a mixer
C. A circulator and a filter operating in a feed-forward loop
D. A filter and an amplifier operating in a feedback loop

(D) To make an oscillator requires an amplifier and a circuit to route some of the amplifier's output signal back to the input (called a feedback loop) such that it is reinforced in the amplifier output. This is called positive feedback. A filter in the feedback loop is used so only signals at the desired frequency are reinforced. Starting with random noise, the oscillator gradually builds up an output signal at the filter frequency until it is self-sustaining. [*General Class License Manual*, page 5-3]

G7B08 **How is the efficiency of an RF power amplifier determined?**

A. Divide the DC input power by the DC output power
B. Divide the RF output power by the DC input power
C. Multiply the RF input power by the reciprocal of the RF output power
D. Add the RF input power to the DC output power

(B) Efficiency is defined as the total output power divided by the total input power and is measured in percent. For an RF amplifier, total output power is measured by a wattmeter. The total input power is the dc power required for the amplifier to operate. For example, if an amplifier requires 1000 mA of plate current at a voltage of 2000 V to produce 1200 watts of RF output, its efficiency = 1200 watts / (1 A × 2000 V) = 1200 / 2000 = 60%. [*General Class License Manual*, page 5-14]

G7B09 **What determines the frequency of an LC oscillator?**

A. The number of stages in the counter
B. The number of stages in the divider
C. The inductance and capacitance in the tank circuit
D. The time delay of the lag circuit

(C) An LC oscillator uses a parallel LC circuit (a tank circuit, which has that name because it stores energy) as the filter in the feedback loop. (See also G7B07.) [*General Class License Manual*, page 5-3]

G7B10 **Which of the following describes a linear amplifier?**

A. Any RF power amplifier used in conjunction with an amateur transceiver
B. An amplifier in which the output preserves the input waveform
C. A Class C high efficiency amplifier
D. An amplifier used as a frequency multiplier

(B) A linear amplifier is defined as one with an output waveform that is a copy of the input waveform, although larger in amplitude. Hams refer to power amplifiers as "linears", whether they are operating linearly (for AM or SSB modes) or not (for CW or FM). It is important to understand when linear operation is important. An amplifier designed for FM will not be suitable as an SSB amplifier, for example. [*General Class License Manual*, page 5-8]

G7B11 **For which of the following modes is a Class C power stage appropriate for amplifying a modulated signal?**

A. SSB
B. FM
C. AM
D. All these choices are correct

(B) A Class C amplifier conducts current during less than half of the input signal cycle, resulting in high distortion. This rules out Class C amplifiers for any form of amplitude modulation, such as SSB or AM. Class C amplifiers can be used for CW since that mode requires only the presence or absence of a signal. Similarly, Class C is suitable for FM signals that only depend on signal frequency, which is not changed by the amplifier. Class C amplifiers generate significant amounts of harmonic energy, so they require filtering when used as transmitter output stages. [*General Class License Manual*, page 5-14]

G7C — Transceiver design; filters; oscillators; digital signal processing (DSP)

G7C01 What circuit is used to select one of the sidebands from a balanced modulator?

A. Carrier oscillator
B. Filter
C. IF amplifier
D. RF amplifier

(B) In a single-sideband transmitter modulating audio can be added to the RF signal by a balanced modulator which also balances out or cancels the original carrier signal. This leaves a double-sideband, suppressed-carrier signal. A filter then removes one of the sidebands, leaving a single-sideband signal that is sent to the mixer, where it combines with the signal from a local oscillator (LO) to produce the RF signal that is amplified and sent to the antenna. The LO shown in the figure is crystal-controlled for fixed-frequency operation. Replacing the crystal-controlled LO with a variable-frequency oscillator (VFO) results in a tunable transmitter similar to those in most modern transceivers. See **Figure G7.6**. [*General Class License Manual*, page 5-8]

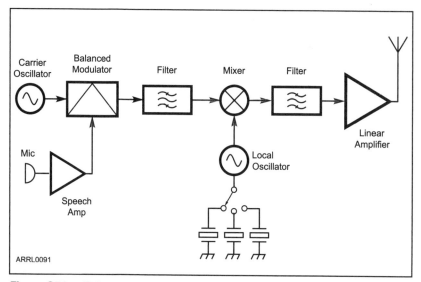

Figure G7.6 — This block diagram shows a basic single-sideband, suppressed-carrier (SSB) transmitter.

G7C02   What output is produced by a balanced modulator?

  A. Frequency modulated RF
  B. Audio with equalized frequency response
  C. Audio extracted from the modulation signal
  D. Double-sideband modulated RF

(D)   See G7C01. [*General Class License Manual*, page 5-8]

G7C03   What is one reason to use an impedance matching transformer at a transmitter output?

  A. To minimize transmitter power output
  B. To present the desired impedance to the transmitter and feed line
  C. To reduce power supply ripple
  D. To minimize radiation resistance

(B)   Special RF *impedance transformers* are often employed to equalize impedances of source and load to maximize the transfer of power. This is a reason to use an impedance matching transformer at the transmitter's output. Impedance-matching can also be performed by special lengths and connections of transmission line. [*General Class License Manual*, page 4-23]

G7C04   How is a product detector used?

  A. Used in test gear to detect spurious mixing products
  B. Used in transmitter to perform frequency multiplication
  C. Used in an FM receiver to filter out unwanted sidebands
  D. Used in a single sideband receiver to extract the modulated signal

(D)   Once amplified to a more usable level, SSB and CW signals are demodulated by a product detector, a special type of mixer. [*General Class License Manual*, page 5-16]

G7C05   Which of the following is characteristic of a direct digital synthesizer (DDS)?

  A. Extremely narrow tuning range
  B. Relatively high-power output
  C. Pure sine wave output
  D. Variable output frequency with the stability of a crystal oscillator

(D)   A direct digital synthesizer or DDS replaces analog VFO circuits by creating a sine wave as a series of small steps. The duration and amplitude of each step is precisely controlled and based on a crystal oscillator. This allows a DDS to act as an oscillator with stability that is comparable to that of a crystal oscillator, while still being adjustable over a wide range. [*General Class License Manual*, page 5-3]

G7C06 **Which of the following is an advantage of a digital signal processing (DSP) filter compared to an analog filter?**

A. A wide range of filter bandwidths and shapes can be created
B. Fewer digital components are required
C. Mixing products are greatly reduced
D. The DSP filter is much more effective at VHF frequencies

(B) DSP technology has two major advantages over analog circuitry — performance and flexibility. Current DSP components can achieve performance as good as or better than the best analog filters. DSP receivers offer selectable preprogrammed filters and allow the operator to adjust the filter bandwidth and shape and even to define new filters. Functions that would be prohibitively expensive in analog circuitry can be implemented in DSP as a program without any additional hardware cost. DSP is limited only by processor speed and available memory as to how many options, functions, and adjustments can be created. [*General Class License Manual*, page 5-16]

G7C07 **What term specifies a filter's attenuation inside its passband?**

A. Insertion loss
B. Return loss
C. Q
D. Ultimate rejection

(A) Even though a filter passes a range of frequencies, it may still attenuate signals in its passband. This is called insertion loss. [*General Class License Manual*, page 5-3]

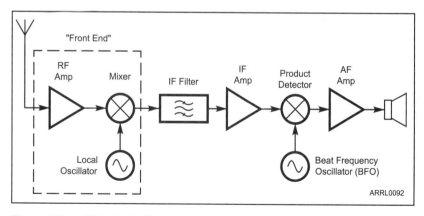

Figure G7.7 — This block diagram shows a simple superheterodyne SSB receiver.

G7C08   **Which parameter affects receiver sensitivity?**

    A. Input amplifier gain
    B. Demodulator stage bandwidth
    C. Input amplifier noise figure
    D. All these choices are correct

(D)   Most analog receivers in use by amateurs today are some type of superheterodyne, a design invented in the 1920s by Edwin Armstrong. As you learned earlier, the mixing together of signals to obtain sum and difference frequencies is called heterodyning. The "superhet" is built around that process.

Received signals are incredibly weak — on the order of nano or picowatts. Thus, a receiver must be quite sensitive to make it possible for an operator to hear such a signal. Simultaneously, a single signal must be picked out of a crowded spectrum where nearby signals might be billions of times stronger. So the receiver must be very selective, as well. Both of these requirements are satisfied by the basic superheterodyne receiver structure shown in Figure G7.8. Let's trace the signal through the receiver from antenna to speaker. [*General Class License Manual*, page 5-16]

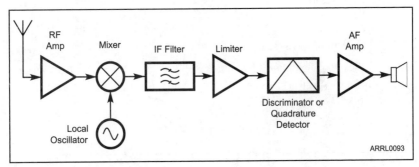

Figure G7.8 — This block diagram shows a simple FM receiver.

G7C09 What is the phase difference between the I and Q RF signals that software-defined radio (SDR) equipment uses for modulation and demodulation?

A. Zero
B. 90 degrees
C. 180 degrees
D. 45 degrees

(B) I refers to in-phase and Q to quadrature. I and Q represent input signals. **Figure G7.9** shows how I/Q modulation works. An RF carrier from a local oscillator (LO) signal is split into two signals, one of which is phase-shifted by 90 degrees. (This is where the word "quadrature" comes from.) The LO signals are applied to a mixer along with the I or Q signal. The result is a pair of modulated signals that are then added together in the combiner stage. The RF output of the combiner consists of a pair of modulated signals that have carrier signals with a 90-degree difference in phase. [*General Class License Manual*, page 5-3]

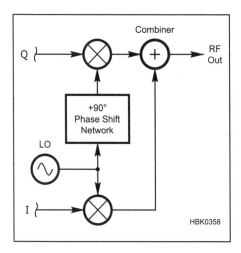

Figure G7.9 — Block diagram of an I/Q modulator. I and Q are input signals that can be analog signals or streams of digital data.

G7C10   What is an advantage of using I-Q modulation signals in software-defined radios (SDRs)?

A. The need for high resolution analog-to-digital converters is eliminated
B. All types of modulation can be created with appropriate processing
C. Minimum detectible signal level is reduced
D. Automatic conversion of the signal from digital to analog

(B)   *Quadrature modulation* is also called *I/Q modulation* because of the I and Q signals that create the modulated output signal. This technique is primarily used to transmit digital data but different combinations of the I and Q signals can create signals with any form of modulation. The technique is particularly well-suited to DSP and is widely used with SDR radios. [*General Class License Manual*, page 5-3]

G7C11   Which of these functions is performed by software in a software-defined radio (SDR)?

A. Filtering
B. Detection
C. Modulation
D. All these choices are correct

(D)   In a software-defined radio (SDR) nearly all of the radio's functions (filtering, detection, modulation, etc.) are performed as digital calculations by software. This allows the radio's operation to be changed and controlled by software without having to change the way in which the radio is physically constructed. [*General Class License Manual*, page 5-3]

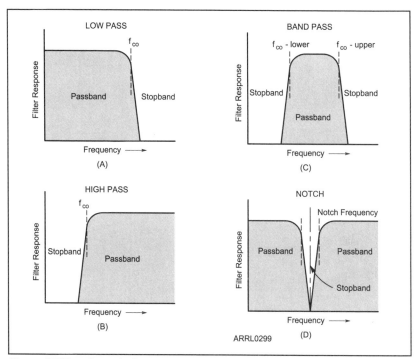

Figure G7.10 — Generic filter response curves showing how filters of different types affect signals. A larger filter response means less attenuation of the signal. Cutoff frequencies are shown as f_{co}.

Subelement G8

Signals and Emissions

[3 Exam Questions — 3 Groups]

G8A — Carriers and modulation: AM, FM, single sideband; modulation envelope; digital modulation; overmodulation; link budgets and link margins

G8A01 How is direct binary FSK modulation generated?
- A. By keying an FM transmitter with a sub-audible tone
- B. By changing an oscillator's frequency directly with a digital control signal
- C. By using a transceiver's computer data interface protocol to change frequencies
- D. By reconfiguring the CW keying input to act as a tone generator

(B) FSK (frequency shift keying) is distinguished from AFSK (audio frequency shift keying) because of the way modulation is performed. AFSK is generated by modulating an SSB transmitter with mark and space audio tones. FSK is often called "direct FSK" to distinguish it from AFSK because a control signal shifts an RF oscillator's frequency with each digital 0 and 1. On the air, properly generated FSK and AFSK are nearly identical. [*General Class License Manual*, page 6-1]

G8A02 **What is the name of the process that changes the phase angle of an RF signal to convey information?**

A. Phase convolution
B. Phase modulation
C. Phase transformation
D. Phase inversion

(B) There are three characteristics of a sine wave which can be varied in order to carry information as modulation: amplitude, frequency, and phase. Phase modulation varies the phase angle of the sine wave with respect to some reference angle as shown in **Figure G8.1**. [*General Class License Manual*, page 5-1]

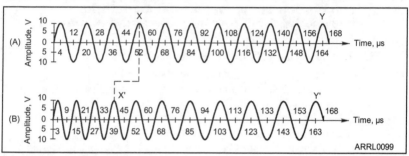

Figure G8.1 — This drawing shows a graphical representation of phase modulation. The unmodulated wave is shown at A. Part B shows the modulated wave. After modulation, cycle X' occurs earlier than cycle X did. All the cycles to the left of X' are compressed, and to the right they are spread out.

G8A03 **What is the name of the process that changes the instantaneous frequency of an RF wave to convey information?**

A. Frequency convolution
B. Frequency transformation
C. Frequency conversion
D. Frequency modulation

(D) See G8A02 and **Figure G8.2**.
[*General Class License Manual*, page 5-1]

Figure G8.2 — This drawing shows a graphical representation of frequency modulation. In the unmodulated carrier at Part A, each RF cycle takes the same amount of time to complete. When the modulating signal of Part B is applied, the carrier frequency is increased or decreased according to the amplitude and polarity of the modulating signal. Part C shows the modulated RF wave.

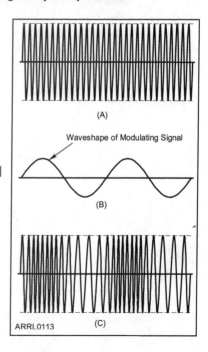

G8A04   **What emission is produced by a reactance modulator connected to a transmitter RF amplifier stage?**

A. Multiplex modulation
B. Phase modulation
C. Amplitude modulation
D. Pulse modulation

(B)   Reactance modulators are the most common method of generating phase modulation (PM) signals. Phase modulators cause the output signal phase to vary with both the modulating signal's amplitude and frequency. (See also G8A02 and **Figure G8.3**.) [*General Class License Manual*, page 5-4]

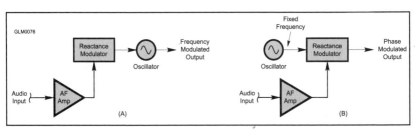

Figure G8.3 — Reactance modulators can be used to create frequency modulation (A) or phase modulation (B).

G8A05   **What type of modulation varies the instantaneous power level of the RF signal?**

A. Power Modulation
B. Phase modulation
C. Frequency modulation
D. Amplitude modulation

(D)   Amplitude modulation (AM) varies the instantaneous amplitude of the RF signal according to the modulating audio signal. (See also G8A02 and **Figure G8.4**.) [*General Class License Manual*, page 5-1]

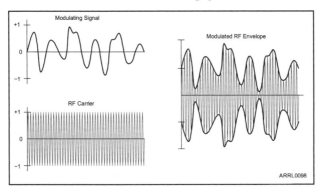

Figure G8.4 — This drawing shows the relationship between the modulating audio waveform, the RF carrier and the resulting RF envelope in a double-sideband, full-carrier amplitude-modulated signal.

G8A06 **Which of the following is characteristic of QPSK31?**

A. It is sideband sensitive
B. Its encoding provides error correction
C. Its bandwidth is approximately the same as BPSK31
D. All these choices are correct

(D) QPSK31 (quadrature phase shift keying) sends two audio tones so that there are four possible phase shift combinations. That allows data to be encoded in a way that provides some error correction to improve performance in noisy conditions. Since there are two tones, you have to select the correct sideband (USB or LSB) to decode the data, meaning the mode is sideband sensitive. QPSK31 and PSK31 have approximately the same bandwidth. [*General Class License Manual*, page 6-4]

G8A07 **Which of the following phone emissions uses the narrowest bandwidth?**

A. Single sideband
B. Double sideband
C. Phase modulation
D. Frequency modulation

(A) In a single-sideband (SSB) amplitude-modulated signal, because the carrier and one sideband are removed, only enough bandwidth is required to transmit a single sideband. The bandwidth of an SSB signal is between about 2 and 3 kHz, the bandwidth of a double-sideband AM signal is about 6 kHz and the bandwidth of frequency and phase modulated phone signals is about 16 kHz. [*General Class License Manual*, page 5-1]

G8A08 **Which of the following is an effect of overmodulation?**

A. Insufficient audio
B. Insufficient bandwidth
C. Frequency drift
D. Excessive bandwidth

(D) When an SSB signal is overmodulated the output waveform of the signal is distorted, which causes spurious emissions outside the normal bandwidth of the signal (**Figure G8.5**). When an FM or PM signal is overmodulated, the deviation of the signal becomes too high and again, spurious emissions appear outside the normal bandwidth of the signal. In both cases, the spurious emissions can cause interference to other stations. [*General Class License Manual*, page 5-8]

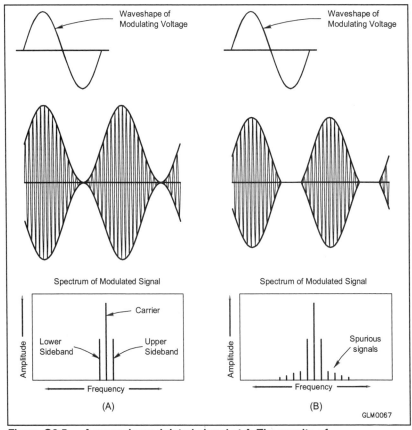

Waveshape of Modulating Voltage

Waveshape of Modulating Voltage

Spectrum of Modulated Signal

Amplitude

Lower Sideband

Carrier

Upper Sideband

Frequency

(A)

Spectrum of Modulated Signal

Amplitude

Spurious signals

Frequency

(B)

GLM0067

Figure G8.5 — A properly modulated signal at A. The results of overmodulation are visible at B. This distorted signal creates spurious emissions which cause interference on nearby frequencies.

G8A09   What type of modulation is used by FT8?

A. 8-tone frequency shift keying
B. Vestigial sideband
C. Amplitude compressed AM
D. 8-bit direct sequence spread spectrum

(A)   Both FT8 and JT65 use precisely timed sequences of transmit and receive, 8-tone FSK modulation, and sophisticated error decoding and correction techniques to enable successful decoding at very low signal-to-noise ratios (SNR). [*General Class License Manual*, page 6-6]

G8A10 What is meant by the term "flat-topping," when referring to an amplitude-modulated phone signal?

    A. Signal distortion caused by insufficient collector current
    B. The transmitter's automatic level control (ALC) is properly adjusted
    C. Signal distortion caused by excessive drive or speech levels
    D. The transmitter's carrier is properly suppressed

(C) **Figure G8.6** shows an overmodulated signal as seen on an oscilloscope with flattening at the maximum levels of the envelope. This is referred to as flat-topping. [*General Class License Manual*, page 5-8]

G8A11 What is the modulation envelope of an AM signal?

    A. The waveform created by connecting the peak values of the modulated signal
    B. The carrier frequency that contains the signal
    C. Spurious signals that envelop nearby frequencies
    D. The bandwidth of the modulated signal

(A) See question G8A05 and **Figure G8.4** for an illustration of an AM waveform's modulation envelope. [*General Class License Manual*, page 5-8]

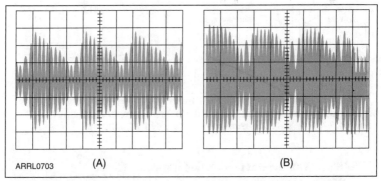

Figure G8.6 — Part A shows the output of a properly adjusted SSB transmitter. Part B shows the effects of overmodulation causing the highest peaks of the waveform to be limited or clipped, often referred to as flat-topping due to the flattening of the waveform envelope at a maximum value.

G8A12   What is QPSK modulation?

A. Modulation using quasi-parallel to serial conversion to reduce bandwidth
B. Modulation using quadra-pole sideband keying to generate spread spectrum signals
C. Modulation using Fast Fourier Transforms to generate frequencies at the first, second, third, and fourth harmonics of the carrier frequency to improve noise immunity
D. Modulation in which digital data is transmitted using 0-, 90-, 180- and 270-degrees phase shift to represent pairs of bits

(D)   While PSK shifts a single signal between two different phases, quadrature phase shift keying shifts two signals between four relative phases (0, 90, 180, and 270 degrees) to represent pairs of bits. FSK and PSK employ error detection methods and an ARQ protocol to insure the reliability of the transferred data. [*General Class License Manual*, page 6-6]

G8A13   What is a link budget?

A. The financial costs associated with operating a radio link
B. The sum of antenna gains minus system losses
C. The sum of transmit power and antenna gains minus system losses as seen at the receiver
D. The difference between transmit power and receiver sensitivity

(C)   A *link budget* is a telecommunications term that accounts for all the power gains and losses a signal experiences within a system. The system can be from your wi-fi router to your computer or from the cable company to your television or from an amateur radio transmitter to a receiver. In amateur radio, this generally boils down to the transmit power and antenna gains from the sending station minus any system losses the receiving station experiences. Losses can result from ionospheric refraction, attenuation, or a variety of other causes. [*General Class License Manual*, page 5-1]

G8A14   What is link margin?

A. The opposite of fade margin
B. The difference between received power level and minimum required signal level at the input to the receiver
C. Transmit power minus receiver sensitivity
D. Receiver sensitivity plus 3 dB

(C)   A *link margin (LKM)* is the difference between the minimum power level needed to receive a signal and the actual power level of the received signal. LKM is measured in dB. [*General Class License Manual*, page 5-1]

G8B — Frequency changing; bandwidths of various modes; deviation; intermodulation

G8B01   Which mixer input is varied or tuned to convert signals of different frequencies to an intermediate frequency (IF)?

A. Image frequency
B. Local oscillator
C. RF input
D. Beat frequency oscillator

(B)   The local oscillator (LO) is adjusted so that the desired signal creates a mixing product at a fixed frequency, called the intermediate frequency (IF). [*General Class License Manual*, page 5-16]

G8B02   What is the term for interference from a signal at twice the IF frequency from the desired signal?

A. Quadrature noise
B. Image response
C. Mixer interference
D. Intermediate interference

(B)   A mixer combines signals from an RF input and a local oscillator (LO) to produce mixing product signals with frequencies that are the sum and difference of the RF and LO signals (**Figure G8.7**). In a superheterodyne receiver, one of the new signals at the intermediate frequency (IF) is further amplified and demodulated. For example, if a 13.795 MHz LO signal is mixed with a 14.25 MHz

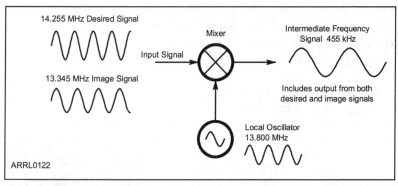

Figure G8.7 — A mixer stage combines an RF input signal with a local oscillator (LO) signal to produce mixing products with frequencies of the sum and difference of the RF and LO frequencies. In a receiver, one of the mixing products at the intermediate frequency (IF) signal is further amplified and demodulated. An undesired signal at the image frequency can also produce a mixing product at the IF, interfering with the desired RF signal.

RF signal, it will result in mixing products at 28.045 MHz and 0.455 MHz, or 455 kHz. A filter then removes the 28.045 MHz signal and passes the 455 kHz signal to the IF amplifier stages. In this case the input signal is 14.255 MHz and the oscillator signal is 13.800 MHz. The mixing products from these two signals are at 28.055 MHz and 0.455 MHz or 455 kHz, which is the intermediate frequency or IF. A signal at 13.455 MHz, when subtracted from the 13.800 MHz oscillator signal will also produce the 455 kHz intermediate frequency. When an undesired input signal also produces a signal at the intermediate frequency, the resulting interference is called image response interference. One way to reduce image response interference is to use an input filter to block signals outside of the desired range. [*General Class License Manual*, page 5-17]

G8B03 **What is another term for the mixing of two RF signals?**

A. Heterodyning
B. Synthesizing
C. Frequency inversion
D. Phase inverting

(A) The process of mixing signals is known as heterodyning. A receiver that mixes a local oscillator (LO) signal with a received RF signal to produce a signal at some intermediate frequency (IF) that is higher in frequency than the baseband audio signal is called a superheterodyne or superhet receiver. The IF signal is processed further by filtering and amplifying it, and then converting the signal to baseband audio. The audio signal is further amplified and fed to a speaker or is connected to headphones so you can hear the received signal. [*General Class License Manual*, page 5-4]

G8B04 **What is the stage in a VHF FM transmitter that generates a harmonic of a lower frequency signal to reach the desired operating frequency?**

A. Mixer
B. Reactance modulator
C. Balanced converter
D. Multiplier

(D) In a VHF FM transmitter, a reactance modulator operates on a radio-frequency oscillator that is normally operating in the high frequency (HF) range. A frequency multiplier doubles or triples the frequency of the modulated signal, usually by generating harmonics of the modulated HF signal and selecting one for output to the next stage in the transmitter. Sometimes several multiplier stages are required to produce a signal at the desired output frequency. [*General Class License Manual*, page 5-4]

G8B05 **Which intermodulation products are closest to the original signal frequencies?**

A. Second harmonics
B. Even-order
C. Odd-order
D. Intercept point

(C)   Harmonics are multiples of a fundamental frequency. So, if the fundamental frequency is 144 MHz, then the second harmonic is 244 MHz, the third is 432 MHz, etc. Note that there is no first harmonic. The first harmonic is the fundamental frequency. [*General Class License Manual*, page 5-22]

G8B06 **What is the total bandwidth of an FM phone transmission having 5 kHz deviation and 3 kHz modulating frequency?**

A. 3 kHz
B. 5 kHz
C. 8 kHz
D. 16 kHz

(D)   To determine bandwidth of an FM-phone transmission, use the following formula, called Carson's Rule:

$$BW = 2 \times (D + M)$$

where:

BW = bandwidth

D = frequency deviation (the instantaneous change in frequency for a given signal)

M = maximum modulating audio frequency

The total bandwidth of an FM phone transmission having a 5 kHz deviation and a 3 kHz modulating frequency would be:

$$2 \times (5 \text{ kHz} + 3 \text{ kHz}) = 16 \text{ kHz}$$

[*General Class License Manual*, page 5-8]

G8B07 What is the frequency deviation for a 12.21 MHz reactance modulated oscillator in a 5 kHz deviation, 146.52 MHz FM phone transmitter?

A. 101.75 Hz
B. 416.7 Hz
C. 5 kHz
D. 60 kHz

(B) See G8B04. When an FM signal's frequency is multiplied, the deviation is also multiplied. This is why the deviation of the modulated oscillator is less than that of the final output signal. To determine the required oscillator frequency deviation, divide the transmitter's output frequency by the oscillator frequency to determine the multiplication factor of the transmitter:

$$\text{Multiplication factor} = \frac{\text{Transmitter output frequency}}{\text{Oscillator frequency}}$$

The multiplication factor for this transmitter is 146.52 MHz / 12.21 MHz = 12. Next divide the desired output deviation by the multiplication factor to obtain the deviation required in the oscillator: 5 kHz / 12 = 416.7 Hz. [*General Class License Manual*, page 5-8]

G8B08 Why is it important to know the duty cycle of the mode you are using when transmitting?

A. To aid in tuning your transmitter
B. Some modes have high duty cycles that could exceed the transmitter's average power rating
C. To allow time for the other station to break in during a transmission
D. To prevent overmodulation

(B) Most Amateur Radio transmitters are not designed to operate at full power output for an extended time. The final output stage is not able to dissipate all of the excess heat generated when the transmitter is continuously producing full output power. When you are operating CW, for example, the transmitter is turned on and off to form the Morse code characters so that the transmitter is only operating at full power about 40 to 50% of the time. During the off times, the amplifier stage cools sufficiently to allow full-power operation. When you are operating single-sideband voice, the transmitter is producing full power only when your voice reaches maximum amplitude. For a typical SSB conversation, the transmitter is operating at full power only about 20 to 25% of the time.

When you are operating some digital modes, however, your transmitter may be operating at full power the entire time you are transmitting. For radioteletype the transmitter is producing full output power, switching between the mark and space tones, so the duty cycle is 100%. For PSK31 and similar modes, the transmitter is producing full power for virtually the entire transmit time, so the duty cycle is 100%. PACTOR, packet radio and a few other modes have slightly reduced duty cycles because the transmitter sends some data and then waits to receive an acknowledgement. If you are operating a high-duty-cycle mode you should reduce your transmit power to prevent overheating the amplifier. Consult your radio's manual to determine the manufacturer's recommendations or reduce power output to 50% or less of full power when operating using a digital mode. [*General Class License Manual*, page 6-12]

G8B09 Why is it good to match receiver bandwidth to the bandwidth of the operating mode?

A. It is required by FCC rules
B. It minimizes power consumption in the receiver
C. It improves impedance matching of the antenna
D. It results in the best signal-to-noise ratio

(D) By matching the receiver bandwidth and the signal bandwidth, noise outside the signal's bandwidth is rejected and no necessary signal energy is discarded. Both result in improvement of the received signal-to-noise ratio (SNR). [*General Class License Manual*, page 5-17]

G8B10 What is the relationship between transmitted symbol rate and bandwidth?

A. Symbol rate and bandwidth are not related
B. Higher symbol rates require wider bandwidth
C. Lower symbol rates require wider bandwidth
D. Bandwidth is half the symbol rate

(B) Advanced modulation techniques can pack multiple bits of data into each transmitted symbol, but it is the symbol rate that sets a minimum limit on bandwidth. Increasing the rate at which symbols are transmitted requires more signal bandwidth in order to maintain a minimum signal-to-noise ratio. [*General Class License Manual*, page 6-12]

G8B11 What combination of a mixer's Local Oscillator (LO) and RF input frequencies is found in the output?

A. The ratio
B. The average
C. The sum and difference
D. The arithmetic product

(C) See G8B03. [*General Class License Manual*, page 5-4]

G8B12   What process combines two signals in a non-linear circuit to produce unwanted spurious outputs?

A. Intermodulation
B. Heterodyning
C. Detection
D. Rolloff

(A)   Nonlinear connections or circuits can act as a mixer and generate mixing products from any signals that are present. [*General Class License Manual*, page 5-22]

G8B13   Which of the following is an odd-order intermodulation product of frequencies F1 and F2?

A. 5F1-3F2
B. 3F1-F2
C. 2F1-F2
D. All these choices are correct

(C)   The following list shows the relationship of first through fifth order harmonics:

f1, f2: 1st order harmonics (fundamental)

f1+f2, f2-f1: 2nd order harmonics

2f1-f2, 2f2-f1: 3rd order harmonics

2f2+2f1, 2f2-2f1: 4th order harmonics

3f1+2f2, 3f2-2f1: 5th order harmonics [*General Class License Manual*, page 5-22]

G8C — Digital emission modes

G8C01   On what band do amateurs share channels with the unlicensed Wi-Fi service?

A. 432 MHz
B. 902 MHz
C. 2.4 GHz
D. 10.7 GHz

(C)   Hams share some spectrum in the 13-centimeter (2.3 GHz) band with Wi-Fi channels and may even use some of the Wi-Fi protocols, but amateurs may not communicate with unlicensed Wi-Fi stations. [*General Class License Manual*, page 3-8]

G8C02 **Which digital mode is used as a low-power beacon for assessing HF propagation?**

A. WSPR
B. MFSK16
C. PSK31
D. SSB-SC

(A) WSPR (pronounced "Whisper") is designed to experiment with and assess HF propagation paths at very low signal-to-noise ratios. WSPR does not support two-way QSOs and acts as a very narrow bandwidth beacon. [*General Class License Manual*, page 6-6]

G8C03 **What part of a packet radio frame contains the routing and handling information?**

A. Directory
B. Preamble
C. Header
D. Trailer

(C) Packet radio and other packetized protocols combine the message to be transferred with control and routing instructions in groups called frames. Each frame is transmitted separately. The entire message is then reassembled at the destination from the received frames. Frames begin with a header that contains information about the routing and handling of the frame. Headers are followed by the data section of the frame and a short terminating segment called the trailer that tells the receiver the frame is complete. Error detection and correction information can also be included in the header or trailer, depending on the protocol being used. [*General Class License Manual*, page 6-6]

G8C04 **Which of the following describes Baudot code?**

A. A 7-bit code with start, stop, and parity bits
B. A code using error detection and correction
C. A 5-bit code with additional start and stop bits
D. A code using SELCAL and LISTEN

(C) The Baudot code used for radioteletype (RTTY) has five data bits per character. This limits the code to $2^5 = 32$ possible characters but special characters (LTRS and FIGS) switch the code between two character sets: capital letters or numbers and punctuation. So the receiver can decode the characters from the transmitted signal, an additional START and STOP bit are transmitted with each character. [*General Class License Manual*, page 6-5]

G8C05 In an ARQ mode, what is meant by a NAK response to a transmitted packet?

A. Request retransmission of the packet
B. Packet was received without error
C. Receiving station connected and ready for transmissions
D. Entire file received correctly

(A) PACTOR is an ARQ mode, meaning "Automatic Repeat reQuest," in which errors in received data generate a NAK response transmission by the receiving station, causing the transmitting station to send the frame again. If the frame is received correctly, an ACK response transmission is made so the transmitter can send the next frame. [*General Class License Manual*, page 6-7]

G8C06 What action results from a failure to exchange information due to excessive transmission attempts when using an ARQ mode?

A. The checksum overflows
B. The connection is dropped
C. Packets will be routed incorrectly
D. Encoding reverts to the default character set

(B) Sometimes conditions are unable to sustain an error-free exchange of data, resulting in repeated NAK responses (see G8C05) that would never stop. To prevent occupying a channel when communications is not possible, either station may decide to terminate the connection between stations when too many NAK responses have been received or transmitted. Connections can also "time out" and be terminated when no frame has been received or the receiver has not responded for a specified time. [*General Class License Manual*, page 6-7]

G8C07 Which of the following narrow-band digital modes can receive signals with very low signal-to-noise ratios?

A. MSK144
B. FT8
C. AMTOR
D. MFSK32

(B) FT8 and WSPR are modes supported by the *WSJT* software suite along with Q65, MSK144, and other digital modes. Both use precisely timed sequences of transmit and receive, 8-tone FSK modulation, and sophisticated error decoding and correction techniques to enable successful decoding at very low signal-to-noise ratios (SNR). WSPR can decode signals at SNR levels approaching –30 dB — a signal 1000 times weaker than the noise! FT8 is very popular because of its excellent performance with modest stations and high noise levels. [*General Class License Manual*, page 6-7]

G8C08   **Which of the following statements is true about PSK31?**

A. Upper case letters are sent with more power
B. Upper case letters use longer Varicode bit sequences and thus slow down transmission
C. Error correction is used to ensure accurate message reception
D. Higher power is needed as compared to RTTY for similar error rates

(B)   In Varicode, the encoding scheme used by PSK31, the most common characters are sent using shorter codes to speed up transmissions. Upper-case letters are less common than lower-case and were assigned longer codes. Thus, unlike RTTY which uses only upper-case letters, capital letters take longer to transmit than lower-case in PSK31. [*General Class License Manual*, page 6-4]

G8C09   **Which is true of mesh network microwave nodes?**

A. Having more nodes increases signal strengths
B. If one node fails, a packet may still reach its target station via an alternate node
C. Links between two nodes in a network may have different frequencies and bandwidths
D. More nodes reduce overall microwave out of band interference

(B)   There are two basic network topologies that hams utilize: mesh (also known as point-to-point or point-to-multipoint) and star configurations. AREDN (Amateur Radio Emergency Data Network), employs a mesh network, while HamWAN, HamNet, and Mi6WAN, employ what is called a star configuration. An advantage of the mesh networking topology is that if one node fails, a packet may be able to find its destination by routing through another available node. [*General Class License Manual*, page 6-7]

G8C10   **How does forward error correction (FEC) allow the receiver to correct data errors?**

A. By controlling transmitter output power for optimum signal strength
B. By using the Varicode character set
C. By transmitting redundant information with the data
D. By using a parity bit with each character

(C)   Forward error correction (FEC) is the practice of sending redundant data in the transmitted frame that allows the receiver to correct some types of errors that may be caused by noise, fading or interference. There are a number of FEC methods involving special codes. [*General Class License Manual*, page 6-7]

G8C11 How are the two separate frequencies of a Frequency Shift Keyed (FSK) signal identified?

A. Dot and dash
B. On and off
C. High and low
D. Mark and space

(D) For an FSK signal that uses two tones (MFSK or multiple-FSK modulation uses more than two tones), a Mark tone represents a digital bit value of 1 and a Space tone represents a 0. [*General Class License Manual*, page 6-1]

G8C12 Which type of code is used for sending characters in a PSK31 signal?

A. Varicode
B. Viterbi
C. Volumetric
D. Binary

(A) Unlike most other digital modes which use fixed-length codes for each transmitted symbol, PSK31 uses a variable-length code called Varicode in which the more common characters use shorter codes to save transmission time, just as Morse code does. [*General Class License Manual*, page 6-4]

G8C13 What is indicated on a waterfall display by one or more vertical lines on either side of a data mode or RTTY signal?

A. Long path propagation
B. Backscatter propagation
C. Insufficient modulation
D. Overmodulation

(D) On a waterfall display like that of **Figure G8.8**, strong signals sometimes seem to have nearby "ghosts" that follow them down the screen, usually as one to three parallel lines. These are distortion products caused by overdriving the transceiver microphone input with the AFSK signals or by the ALC system distorting the RF signal as it changes transmitter power levels. You can get rid of these unwanted spurious emissions by reducing audio levels and setting power levels so that the ALC system is not activated. [*General Class License Manual*, page 6-12]

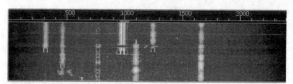

Figure G8.8 — A waterfall display shows signal strength and frequency as a series of lines moving down the display.

G8C14   Which of the following describes a waterfall display?

A. Frequency is horizontal, signal strength is vertical, time is intensity
B. Frequency is vertical, signal strength is intensity, time is horizontal
C. Frequency is horizontal, signal strength is intensity, time is vertical
D. Frequency is vertical, signal strength is horizontal, time is intensity

(C)   A waterfall display is composed of lines which show signal strength across a band of frequencies as intensity or color. As each new scan is displayed, the older lines move down, giving the impression of a waterfall. The most common waterfall display shows frequency horizontally although a few programs have the option of setting the display to "move" horizontally. [*General Class License Manual*, page 6-14]

G8C15   What does an FT8 signal report of +3 mean?

A. The signal is 3 times the noise level of an equivalent SSB signal
B. The signal is S3 (weak signals)
C. The signal-to-noise ratio is equivalent to +3dB in a 2.5 kHz bandwidth
D. The signal is 3 dB over S9

(C)   FT8 exchanges 75-bit messages (plus 12 bits for error detection codes) in a 50 Hz bandwidth. As FT8 is used today, there is a limited amount of information that can be exchanged, such as call signs, grid locators, and signal reports. Signal reports in FT8 are on the signal-to-noise ratio, so a report of +3 means the signal is 3dB above the noise floor. Most frequently, you will find amateurs using FT8 between 14.074 and 14.077 MHz. [*General Class License Manual*, page 6-7]

G8C16   Which of the following provide digital voice modes?

A. WSPR, MFSK16, and EasyPAL
B. FT8, FT4, and FST4
C. Winlink, PACTOR II, and PACTOR III
D. DMR, D-STAR, and SystemFusion

(D)   Digital voice modes are regulated as voice emissions by the FCC. This includes modes such as Icom's D-STAR, Yaesu's System Fusion, AOR's digital voice system, DMR, and the public domain FreeDV. Slow-scan TV is also converting from the analog system to digital file transfer systems that are regulated as image modes. *The ARRL Handbook* reviews these modes in greater detail. [*General Class License Manual*, page 6-16]

Antennas and Feed Lines

[4 Exam Questions — 4 Groups]

G9A — Feed lines: characteristic impedance and attenuation; standing wave ratio (SWR) calculation, measurement, and effects; antenna feed point matching

G9A01   Which of the following factors determine the characteristic impedance of a parallel conductor feed line?

A. The distance between the centers of the conductors and the radius of the conductors

B. The distance between the centers of the conductors and the length of the line

C. The radius of the conductors and the frequency of the signal

D. The frequency of the signal and the length of the line

(A)   The characteristic impedance of a parallel-conductor feed line (**Figure G9.1**) depends on the distance between the conductor centers and the radius of the conductors. [*General Class License Manual*, page 7-20]

G9A02   What is the relationship between high standing wave ratio (SWR) and transmission line loss?

A. There is no relationship between transmission line loss and SWR

B. High SWR increases loss in a lossy transmission line

C. High SWR makes it difficult to measure transmission line loss

D. High SWR reduces the relative effect of transmission line loss

(B)   As SWR increases, more power is reflected by the load. That reflected power must travel through the line and on each round trip, some of it is dissipated as heat due to feed line loss. Thus, increasing SWR in a feed line also increases the total loss in the line. [*General Class License Manual,* page 7-19]

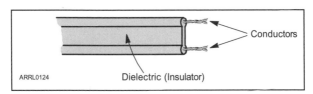

Figure G9.1 — The construction of common 300-ohm twin lead — one form of parallel-conductor feed line.

G9A03 What is the nominal characteristic impedance of "window line" transmission line?

A. 50 ohms
B. 75 ohms
C. 100 ohms
D. 450 ohms

(D) The most common type of parallel-conductor line is window line that has solid plastic insulation between the conductors with rectangular "windows" cut out of the insulation to reduce loss and weight. The typical impedance for window line is 450 Ω although there are several variations as low as 400 Ω. [*General Class License Manual*, page 7-20]

G9A04 What causes reflected power at an antenna's feed point?

A. Operating an antenna at its resonant frequency
B. Using more transmitter power than the antenna can handle
C. A difference between feed line impedance and antenna feed point impedance
D. Feeding the antenna with unbalanced feed line

(C) Whenever power traveling along a feed line encounters a different impedance from the characteristic impedance of the feed line, such as at an antenna, some of the power is reflected back toward the power source. The greater the difference between the feed line's characteristic impedance and the new impedance, the larger the fraction of power that is reflected. [*General Class License Manual*, page 7-20]

G9A05 How does the attenuation of coaxial cable change with increasing frequency?

A. Attenuation is independent of frequency
B. Attenuation increases
C. Attenuation decreases
D. Attenuation follows Marconi's Law of Attenuation

(B) Feed line loss is greater at higher frequencies. For example, if you were to use the same type of coaxial cable for your 160 meter antenna as for your 2 meter antenna, there would be much more loss at the higher 2 meter frequencies. [*General Class License Manual*, page 7-20]

G9A06   **In what units is RF feed line loss usually expressed?**

A. Ohms per 1,000 feet
B. Decibels per 1,000 feet
C. Ohms per 100 feet
D. Decibels per 100 feet

(D)   RF feed line loss is normally specified in decibels of loss for 100 feet of line. Because it changes with frequency, loss is also specified at a certain frequency [*General Class License Manual*, page 7-20]

G9A07   **What must be done to prevent standing waves on a feed line connected to an antenna?**

A. The antenna feed point must be at DC ground potential
B. The feed line must be an odd number of electrical quarter wavelengths long
C. The feed line must be an even number of physical half wavelengths long
D. The antenna feed point impedance must be matched to the characteristic impedance of the feed line

(D)   To eliminate reflected power, the antenna impedance must be matched to the characteristic impedance of the feed line. If the impedances are matched, all of the feed line power is transferred to the antenna. [*General Class License Manual*, page 7-20]

G9A08   **If the SWR on an antenna feed line is 5:1, and a matching network at the transmitter end of the feed line is adjusted to present a 1:1 SWR to the transmitter, what is the resulting SWR on the feed line?**

A. 1:1
B. 5:1
C. Between 1:1 and 5:1 depending on the characteristic impedance of the line
D. Between 1:1 and 5:1 depending on the reflected power at the transmitter

(B)   A matching network at the transmitter does not change the SWR on the feed line, so the feed line SWR is still 5:1. [*General Class License Manual*, page 7-20]

G9A09 What standing wave ratio results from connecting a 50-ohm feed line to a 200-ohm resistive load?

A. 4:1
B. 1:4
C. 2:1
D. 1:2

(A) If a load connected to a feed line is purely resistive, the SWR can be calculated by dividing the line characteristic impedance by the load resistance or vice versa, whichever gives a value greater than one. 200 / 50 = 4:1 SWR. [*General Class License Manual*, page 7-20]

G9A10 What standing wave ratio results from connecting a 50-ohm feed line to a 10-ohm resistive load?

A. 2:1
B. 1:2
C. 1:5
D. 5:1

(D) If a load connected to a feed line is purely resistive, the SWR can be calculated by dividing the line characteristic impedance by the load resistance or vice versa, whichever gives a value greater than one. 50 / 10 = 5:1 SWR. [*General Class License Manual*, page 7-20]

G9A11 What is the effect of transmission line loss on SWR measured at the input to the line?

A. Higher loss reduces SWR measured at the input to the line
B. Higher loss increases SWR measured at the input to the line
C. Higher loss increases the accuracy of SWR measured at the input to the line
D. Transmission line loss does not affect the SWR measurement

(A) SWR is almost always measured at the transmitter end of an antenna feed line. The SWR is calculated by measuring the forward power (PF) and reflected power (PR). (See question G4B10 for the exact formula.) If power reflected from the antenna is lost in the feed line before it reaches the measurement point at the transmitter end, it will appear that less was reflected from the antenna, reducing the measured value of SWR. [*General Class License Manual*, page 7-20]

G9B — Basic dipole and monopole antennas

G9B01   **What is a characteristic of a random-wire HF antenna connected directly to the transmitter?**
A. It must be longer than 1 wavelength
B. Station equipment may carry significant RF current
C. It produces only vertically polarized radiation
D. It is more effective on the lower HF bands than on the higher bands

(B)   A random-wire antenna is connected directly to the transmitter at one end. It can be of any length because an antenna tuner is used to match the impedance of the antenna. There is no feed line. One significant disadvantage of a random-wire antenna is that you may experience RF "hot spots" in your station because the station equipment and wiring are part of your antenna system! [*General Class License Manual*, page 7-16]

G9B02   **Which of the following is a common way to adjust the feed point impedance of an elevated quarter-wave ground-plane vertical antenna to be approximately 50 ohms?**
A. Slope the radials upward
B. Slope the radials downward
C. Lengthen the radials beyond one wavelength
D. Coil the radials

(B)   A ground-plane antenna is often constructed with a ¼-wavelength vertical radiating element and four ¼-wavelength horizontal "radial" wires that form the ground plane. You can change the impedance of a ground-plane antenna by changing the angle of the radials. Bending or sloping the radials downward to about a 45-degree angle will increase the impedance from approximately 35 ohms to approximately 50 ohms which is a better match to most coaxial feed lines. See **Figure G9.2**. [*General Class License Manual*, page 7-1]

Figure G9.2 — A ground-plane antenna may use horizontal (A) or downward-sloping radials. By sloping the radials down (B), the feed point impedance is raised closer to 50 ohms, presenting a better impedance match to 50-ohm coaxial cable.

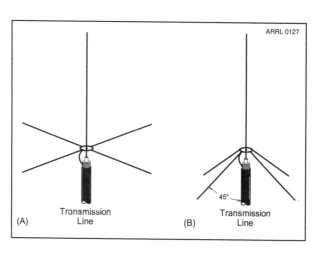

G9B03 **Which of the following best describes the radiation pattern of a quarter-wave, ground-plane vertical antenna?**

A. Bi-directional in azimuth
B. Isotropic
C. Hemispherical
D. Omnidirectional in azimuth

(D) Ground-planes are often called "verticals" because that is the usual way of constructing and installing them. Like a dipole, the ground-plane radiates best broadside to its axis. If installed vertically, this means the ground-plane antenna's pattern is omnidirectional, uniform in all azimuth angles or directions. [*General Class License Manual*, page 7-1]

G9B04 **What is the radiation pattern of a dipole antenna in free space in a plane containing the conductor?**

A. It is a figure-eight at right angles to the antenna
B. It is a figure-eight off both ends of the antenna
C. It is a circle (equal radiation in all directions)
D. It has a pair of lobes on one side of the antenna and a single lobe on the other side

(A) A ½-wavelength dipole antenna radiates its signals in a bi-directional fashion with maximum radiation at right-angles to the antenna, as shown in **Figure G9.3**. This is called a "figure 8" radiation pattern. [*General Class License Manual*, page 7-1]

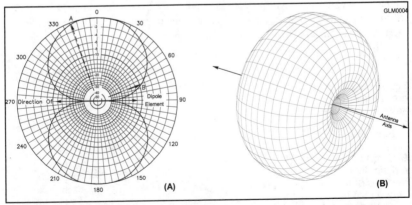

Figure G9.3 — Part A shows the radiation pattern in the plane of a dipole located in free space. The dipole element is located on the line from 270 to 90 degrees in this figure. Part B shows the three-dimensional radiation pattern in all directions around the dipole.

G9B05 How does antenna height affect the azimuthal radiation pattern of a horizontal dipole HF antenna at elevation angles higher than about 45 degrees?

A. If the antenna is too high, the pattern becomes unpredictable
B. Antenna height has no effect on the pattern
C. If the antenna is less than ½ wavelength high, the azimuthal pattern is almost omnidirectional
D. If the antenna is less than ½ wavelength high, radiation off the ends of the wire is eliminated

(C) As height is reduced below ½-wavelength the antenna pattern of the dipole becomes almost omnidirectional because of reflections from the ground. This antenna transmits and receives nearly equally in all compass directions although at a high vertical angle. [*General Class License Manual*, page 7-2]

G9B06 Where should the radial wires of a ground-mounted vertical antenna system be placed?

A. As high as possible above the ground
B. Parallel to the antenna element
C. On the surface or buried a few inches below the ground
D. At the center of the antenna

(C) In most installations, the soil is too lossy to act as an effective ground plane, so an artificial ground screen must be made from radial wires placed on the ground near the base of the antenna. These radials are usually ¼ wavelength or longer (they are not resonant). Depending on ground conductivity, 8, 16, 32 or more radials may be required to form an effective ground. The radial wires of a ground-mounted vertical antenna should be placed on the Earth's surface or buried a few inches below the surface. [*General Class License Manual*, page 7-2]

G9B07 How does the feed point impedance of a horizontal ½ wave dipole antenna change as the antenna height is reduced to 1/10 wavelength above ground?

A. It steadily increases
B. It steadily decreases
C. It peaks at about ⅛ wavelength above ground
D. It is unaffected by the height above ground

(B) As the antenna is lowered below ¼ wavelength above ground, the impedance steadily decreases to a very low value when placed directly on the ground. [*General Class License Manual*, page 7-2]

G9B08 How does the feed point impedance of a ½ wave dipole change as the feed point is moved from the center toward the ends?

A. It steadily increases
B. It steadily decreases
C. It peaks at about ⅛ wavelength from the end
D. It is unaffected by the location of the feed point

(A) The center of a ½-wavelength dipole is the location of the lowest feed point impedance, approximately 72 ohms in free space. At the ends of the dipole, feed point impedance is several thousand ohms. In between, feed point impedance increases steadily as the feed point is moved from the center toward the ends of the antenna. [*General Class License Manual*, page 7-2]

G9B09 Which of the following is an advantage of a horizontally polarized as compared to a vertically polarized HF antenna?

A. Lower ground reflection losses
B. Lower feed point impedance
C. Shorter radials
D. Lower radiation resistance

(A) The signals from a horizontally polarized antenna have lower losses when reflecting from the ground. This is because the horizontal polarization of the wave induces currents that flow along the surface of the ground. Vertical polarization tends to induce currents that flow vertically in the ground, where losses are higher.

Radio waves reflecting from the ground have lower losses when the polarization of the wave is parallel to the ground. That is, when the waves are horizontally polarized. Because the reflected waves combine with the direct waves (not reflected) to make up the antenna's radiation pattern, lower reflection loss results in stronger signal strength.

Ground-mounted vertical antennas, however, are able to generate stronger signals at low angles of radiation than horizontally polarized antennas at low heights. This means they are often preferred for DX contacts on the lower HF bands where it is impractical to raise horizontally polarized antennas to the height necessary for strong low-angle signals. [*General Class License Manual*, page 7-2]

G9B10   **What is the approximate length for a ½ wave dipole antenna cut for 14.250 MHz?**

A. 8 feet
B. 16 feet
C. 24 feet
D. 33 feet

(D)   In free space, ½ wavelength in feet equals 492 divided by frequency in MHz. If you cut a piece of wire that length, however, you'll find it is too long to resonate at the desired frequency. A resonant ½-wave dipole made of ordinary wire will be shorter than the free-space wavelength for several reasons. First, the physical thickness of the wire makes it look a bit longer electrically than it is physically. The thicker the wire or the lower its length-to-diameter (l/d) ratio, the shorter it will be when it is resonant. Second, the dipole's height above ground also affects its resonant frequency. In addition, nearby conductors, insulation on the wire, the means by which the wire is secured to the insulators and to the feed line also affect the resonant length. For these reasons, a single universal formula for dipole length, such as the common 468/f, is not very useful. You should start with a length near the free-space length and be prepared to trim the dipole to resonance using an SWR meter or antenna analyzer. The exam only requires that you identify an approximate resonant length for a dipole. Use the free-space length, calculated as 492 / f (in MHz), and select the closest choice. In this case, length (feet) = 492 / 14.250 = 34.5 feet, so select the closest value — 33 feet. [*General Class License Manual*, page 7-2]

G9B11   **What is the approximate length for a ½ wave dipole antenna cut for 3.550 MHz?**

A. 42 feet
B. 84 feet
C. 132 feet
D. 263 feet

(C)   (See also G9B10.) Calculate length (feet) = 492 / 3.550 = 139 ft. The closest value is 132 feet. [*General Class License Manual*, page 7-2]

G9B12   **What is the approximate length for a ¼ wave monopole antenna cut for 28.5 MHz?**

A. 8 feet
B. 11 feet
C. 16 feet
D. 21 feet

(A)   (See also G9B10.) A ¼-wavelength antenna would be half as long as a ½-wavelength antenna so calculate length (feet) = 246 / 28.5 = 8.6 ft. The closest value is 8 feet. [*General Class License Manual*, page 7-2]

G9C — Directional antennas

G9C01 Which of the following would increase the bandwidth of a Yagi antenna?

A. Larger-diameter elements
B. Closer element spacing
C. Loading coils in series with the element
D. Tapered-diameter elements

(A) Using larger diameter elements increases the SWR bandwidth of a parasitic beam antenna, such as a Yagi antenna as shown in **Figure G9.4**. The exact length of the elements becomes less critical when larger diameter elements are used. [*General Class License Manual*, page 7-8]

G9C02 What is the approximate length of the driven element of a Yagi antenna?

A. ¼ wavelength
B. ½ wavelength
C. ¾ wavelength
D. 1 wavelength

(B) A Yagi antenna consists of a driven element that is close to ½-wavelength long with one or more parasitic elements that help direct the radiated energy in one direction. Directors are parasitic elements that are mounted along the antenna's supporting boom in the preferred direction of radiation and reflectors are mounted in the opposite direction. [*General Class License Manual*, page 7-8]

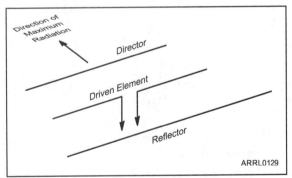

Figure G9.4 — A typical three-element Yagi antenna showing the relative lengths of the elements and the direction of the antenna's main lobe.

G9C03 **How do the lengths of a three-element Yagi reflector and director compare to that of the driven element?**

A. The reflector is longer, and the director is shorter
B. The reflector is shorter, and the director is longer
C. They are all the same length
D. Relative length depends on the frequency of operation

(**A**)   A Yagi's elements are physically arranged to create gain in a single major or main lobe and cancel signals in the opposite direction. The parasitic elements placed in the direction of maximum gain are called directors and are slightly shorter than the driven element. Parasitic elements in the direction of minimum gain are called reflectors and are slightly longer than the driven element. [*General Class License Manual*, page 7-8]

G9C04 **How does antenna gain in dBi compare to gain stated in dBd for the same antenna?**

A. Gain in dBi is 2.15 dB lower
B. Gain in dBi is 2.15 dB higher
C. Gain in dBd is 1.25 dBd lower
D. Gain in dBd is 1.25 dBd higher

(**B**)   The gain of the reference dipole with respect to the isotropic antenna is 2.15 dB. To convert gain from dBd to dBi, add 2.15 dB. [*General Class License Manual*, page 7-8]

G9C05 **What is the primary effect of increasing boom length and adding directors to a Yagi antenna?**

A. Gain increases
B. Beamwidth increases
C. Front-to-back ratio decreases
D. Resonant frequency is lower

(**A**)   As the boom length of a Yagi is increased and more elements are added, the directivity or gain of the antenna increases. Directivity has an advantage in that it concentrates the transmitted and received signals in the intended direction more than in other directions, thus minimizing interference and improving the signal-to-noise ratio of received signals. [*General Class License Manual*, page 7-2]

G9C06 **[Deleted]**

G9C07 **What does "front-to-back ratio" mean in reference to a Yagi antenna?**

A. The number of directors versus the number of reflectors
B. The relative position of the driven element with respect to the reflectors and directors
C. The power radiated in the major lobe compared to that in the opposite direction
D. The ratio of forward gain to dipole gain

(C) Using a directional antenna helps reduce interference in that it sends and receives better in the intended direction rather than off to the side or rear. Most of the radiated signal is sent in the desired direction. If you measure the power radiated in the desired direction and compare it with the power radiated in the exactly opposite direction, that is the antenna's front-to-back ratio as shown in **Figure G9.5**. [*General Class License Manual*, page 7-8]

G9C08 **What is meant by the "main lobe" of a directive antenna?**

A. The magnitude of the maximum vertical angle of radiation
B. The point of maximum current in a radiating antenna element
C. The maximum voltage standing wave point on a radiating element
D. The direction of maximum radiated field strength from the antenna

(D) A Yagi antenna radiates most of the signal in one direction. The range of directions in which the Yagi radiates and receives most strongly is called the main lobe of the antenna's radiation pattern. [*General Class License Manual*, page 7-8]

Figure G9.5 — The directive pattern for a typical three-element Yagi antenna. Note that this pattern is essentially unidirectional, with most of the radiation in the direction of the main lobe. There is also a small minor lobe at 180° from the direction of the main lobe, however. You can read the front-to-back-ratio on this type of graph by finding the strength of the minor lobe off the back of the antenna. For this antenna, the front-to-back-ratio is 24 dB because the maximum signal at 180° just touches the –24 dB circle. That means the signal off the back of the antenna is 24 dB less than the signal from the front or forward direction of the antenna.

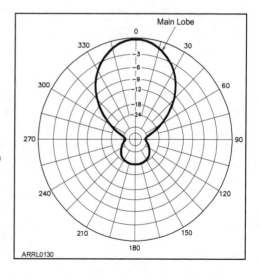

G9C09 In free space, how does the gain of two three-element, horizontally polarized Yagi antennas spaced vertically ½ wavelength apart typically compare to the gain of a single three-element Yagi?

A. Approximately 1.5 dB higher
B. Approximately 3 dB higher
C. Approximately 6 dB higher
D. Approximately 9 dB higher

(B) Called vertical stacking, placing antennas one above the other provides additional focusing of the antenna's radiation pattern, increasing overall gain of the antenna system. A stack of two such antennas doubles gain which is equivalent to a 3 dB increase. [*General Class License Manual*, page 7-16]

G9C10 Which of the following can be adjusted to optimize forward gain, front-to-back ratio, or SWR bandwidth of a Yagi antenna?

A. The physical length of the boom
B. The number of elements on the boom
C. The spacing of each element along the boom
D. All these choices are correct

(D) All of these choices affect a Yagi antenna's forward gain, front-to-back ratio and SWR bandwidth. As you might imagine, adjusting an antenna design for the desired combination of these three important parameters can be a complicated procedure. Computer modeling programs greatly simplify this process. [*General Class License Manual*, page 7-8]

G9C11 What is a beta or hairpin match?

A. A shorted transmission line stub placed at the feed point of a Yagi antenna to provide impedance matching
B. A ¼ wavelength section of 75-ohm coax in series with the feed point of a Yagi to provide impedance matching
C. A series capacitor selected to cancel the inductive reactance of a folded dipole antenna
D. section of 300-ohm twin-lead transmission line used to match a folded dipole antenna

(A) The beta match is a short length or "stub" of parallel conductor transmission line connected directly across the driven element feed point. The stub acts as an inductive reactance that can compensate for any capacitive reactance at the feed point. A balun is used to maintain electrical balance between both halves of the driven element. [*General Class License Manual*, page 7-9]

G9C12 Which of the following is a characteristic of using a gamma match with a Yagi antenna?

A. It does not require the driven element to be insulated from the boom
B. It does not require any inductors or capacitors
C. It is useful for matching multiband antennas
D. All these choices are correct

(A) One major advantage of the gamma match (**Figure G9.6A** and **B**) is that the driven element does not have to be insulated from the antenna's boom. This simplifies the construction and mounting of the driven element. [*General Class License Manual*, page 7-9]

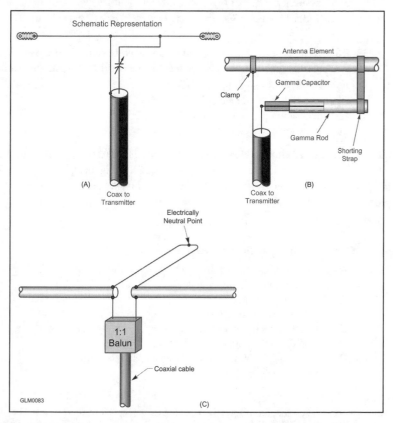

Figure G9.6 — The gamma match (A and B) is a short section of transmission line that transforms a low impedance at the center of the driven element to a higher impedance closer to that of coaxial cable. The gamma match is tuned with the gamma capacitor and by moving the shorting strap. A is the schematic equivalent and B shows typical gamma match construction. C shows the beta or "hairpin" match. The beta match maintains driven element balance. The center point of the stub or hairpin is electrically neutral and can be connected directly to the antenna boom for mechanical stability.

G9D — Specialized antenna types and applications

G9D01   Which of the following antenna types will be most effective as a near vertical incidence skywave (NVIS) antenna for short-skip communications on 40 meters during the day?

   A. A horizontal dipole placed between ¹⁄₁₀ and ¼ wavelength above the ground

   B. A vertical antenna placed between ¼ and ½ wavelength above the ground

   C. Horizontal dipole placed at approximately ½ wavelength above the ground

   D. A vertical dipole placed at approximately ½ wavelength above the ground

(A)   NVIS, or Near Vertical Incidence Skywave, refers to a communications system that uses low, horizontally polarized antennas such as dipoles that radiate most of their signal at high vertical angles. These signals are then reflected back to Earth in a region centered on the antenna. NVIS allows stations to communicate within the skip zone that exists for lower-angle sky wave propagation. [*General Class License Manual*, page 7-2]

G9D02   What is the feed point impedance of an end-fed half-wave antenna?

   A. Very low

   B. Approximately 50 ohms

   C. Approximately 300 ohms

   D. Very high

(D)   Feed point impedance of a ½-wavelength dipole increases as the feed point is moved away from the center and is several thousand ohms at the ends. The end-fed half-wave (EFHW) antenna with its feed point at one end is popular for portable operating because it is lightweight and easy to install. [*General Class License Manual*, page 7-2]

G9D03   In which direction is the maximum radiation from a VHF/UHF "halo" antenna?

   A. Broadside to the plane of the halo

   B. Opposite the feed point

   C. Omnidirectional in the plane of the halo

   D. On the same side as the feed point

(C)   The halo antenna is a dipole bent into a circle or square (the "squalo") with the ends separated by a small gap. The halo radiates most strongly in the plane of the antenna. Halos are usually mounted horizontally so they produce an omnidirectional pattern with the horizontal polarization preferred for VHF weak-signal operation. [*General Class License Manual*, page 7-13]

G9D04 **What is the primary function of antenna traps?**

A. To enable multiband operation
B. To notch spurious frequencies
C. To provide balanced feed-point impedance
D. To prevent out-of-band operation

(A) Traps are parallel LC circuits that act as electrical switches at their resonant frequencies to isolate sections of the antenna. At other frequencies, traps act as inductance or capacitance. This changes the antenna's "electrical length" automatically, allowing it to operate on two or more bands. [*General Class License Manual*, page 7-13]

G9D05 **What is an advantage of vertical stacking of horizontally polarized Yagi antennas?**

A. It allows quick selection of vertical or horizontal polarization
B. It allows simultaneous vertical and horizontal polarization
C. It narrows the main lobe in azimuth
D. It narrows the main lobe in elevation

(D) The increase in gain for a vertical stack of Yagi antennas results from narrowing the vertical width of the main lobe of a single antenna's radiation pattern. The narrower lobe results in stronger received signals and less received noise at angles away from the peak of the main lobe. [*General Class License Manual*, page 7-16]

G9D06 **Which of the following is an advantage of a log-periodic antenna?**

A. Wide bandwidth
B. Higher gain per element than a Yagi antenna
C. Harmonic suppression
D. Polarization diversity

(A) A log-periodic antenna is designed to provide consistent gain and feed point impedance over a wide frequency range. [*General Class License Manual*, page 7-16]

G9D07 **Which of the following describes a log-periodic antenna?**

A. Element length and spacing vary logarithmically along the boom
B. Impedance varies periodically as a function of frequency
C. Gain varies logarithmically as a function of frequency
D. SWR varies periodically as a function of boom length

(A) The name "log periodic" refers to the ratio of length and spacing between adjacent elements of the antenna. By designing the antenna entirely in terms of ratios, the antenna's performance becomes independent of frequency over a wide range. [*General Class License Manual*, page 7-16]

G9D08 **How does a "screwdriver" mobile antenna adjust its feed-point impedance?**

A. By varying its body capacitance
B. By varying the base loading inductance
C. By extending and retracting the whip
D. By deploying a capacitance hat

(B) The "screwdriver" antenna design — a whip with an adjustable loading coil at the base — has gained popularity for HF mobile operation as a good compromise between performance and convenience. The name derives from the small dc motors typical of electric screwdrivers used to adjust the loading coil. [*General Class License Manual*, page 7-2]

G9D09 **What is the primary use of a Beverage antenna?**

A. Directional receiving for MF and low HF bands
B. Directional transmitting for low HF bands
C. Portable direction finding at higher HF frequencies
D. Portable direction finding at lower HF frequencies

(A) Beverage antennas are most effective at frequencies of 7 MHz and below. This includes the amateur MF (medium frequency) 160 meter band, as well as the lower HF bands of 80, 60, and 40 meters. [*General Class License Manual*, page 7-16]

G9D10 **In which direction or directions does an electrically small loop (less than ¹/₁₀ wavelength in circumference) have nulls in its radiation pattern?**

A. In the plane of the loop
B. Broadside to the loop
C. Broadside and in the plane of the loop
D. Electrically small loops are omnidirectional

(B) If the circumference of a loop is less than ⅓ wavelength, current in the loop becomes relatively uniform all the way around the loop. This results in a radiation pattern with sharp nulls broadside to the plane of the loop. [*General Class License Manual*, page 7-13]

G9D11 **Which of the following is a disadvantage of multiband antennas?**

A. They present low impedance on all design frequencies
B. They must be used with an antenna tuner
C. They must be fed with open wire line
D. They have poor harmonic rejection

(D) Multiband antennas by definition are designed to radiate well on several frequencies. Most HF amateur bands are harmonically-related, meaning their frequencies are integer multiples of each other — 3.5, 7, 14, 21, and 28 MHz. While this is convenient in that one antenna can be used on separate bands, harmonics of a fundamental signal on, for example 7 MHz, will be radiated well by a multiband antenna on 14, 21, and 28 MHz. [*General Class License Manual*, page 7-16]

G9D12 **What is the common name of a dipole with a single central support?**

A. Inverted V
B. Inverted L
C. Sloper
D. Lazy H

(A) A dipole needn't be straight to be effective. Using a single antenna support, a dipole supported in the center makes it easy to attach the feed line. This configuration is called an "inverted V." [*General Class License Manual*, page 7-2]

G9D13 **[Deleted]**

Subelement G0

Electrical and RF Safety

[2 Exam Questions — 2 Groups]

G0A — RF safety principles, rules, and guidelines; routine station evaluation

G0A01 What is one way that RF energy can affect human body tissue?

A. It heats body tissue
B. It causes radiation poisoning
C. It causes the blood count to reach a dangerously low level
D. It cools body tissue

(A) Body tissues subjected to very high levels of RF energy may suffer heat damage. These effects depend on the frequency of the energy, the power density of the RF field that strikes the body, and even on factors such as the polarization of the wave. The thermal effects of RF energy should not be a major concern for most radio amateurs because of the relatively low RF power we normally use and the intermittent nature of most amateur transmissions. It is rare for amateurs to be subjected to RF fields strong enough to produce thermal effects unless they are fairly close to an energized antenna or unshielded power amplifier. [*General Class License Manual*, page 9-8]

G0A02 Which of the following is used to determine RF exposure from a transmitted signal?

A. Its duty cycle
B. Its frequency
C. Its power density
D. All these choices are correct

(D) The body's natural resonant frequencies affect how the body absorbs RF energy. For this reason, polarization, power density and the frequency of the radio signal are all important in estimating the effects of RF energy on body tissue. [*General Class License Manual*, page 9-8]

G0A03 How can you determine that your station complies with FCC RF exposure regulations?

A. By calculation based on FCC OET Bulletin 65
B. By calculation based on computer modeling
C. By measurement of field strength using calibrated equipment
D. All these choices are correct

(D) You may use any of these three procedures to determine whether your station complies with the exposure guidelines. The simplest, by far, is to perform the calculations in FCC OET Bulletin 65. There are online and software tools to help you perform the calculations. In complex or unique situations, it may be required to model or measure the exposure. [97.13(c)(1)] [*General Class License Manual*, page 9-8]

G0A04 What does "time averaging" mean when evaluating RF radiation exposure?

A. The average amount of power developed by the transmitter over a specific 24-hour period
B. The average time it takes RF radiation to have any long-term effect on the body
C. The total time of the exposure
D. The total RF exposure averaged over a certain period

(D) Time averaging, when applied to RF radiation exposure, takes into account the total RF exposure by averaging it over either a 6-minute or a 30-minute exposure time. Time averaging compensates for the transmit/receive time ratio during normal amateur communications. It takes into account that the body cools itself after a time of reduced or no RF radiation exposure. [*General Class License Manual*, page 9-9]

G0A05 What must you do if an evaluation of your station shows that the RF energy radiated by your station exceeds permissible limits for possible human absorption?

A. Take action to prevent human exposure to the excessive RF fields
B. File an Environmental Impact Statement (EIS-97) with the FCC
C. Secure written permission from your neighbors to operate above the controlled MPE limits
D. All these choices are correct

(A) Some of the things you can do to prevent human exposure to excessive RF radiation are to move your antennas farther away, restrict access to the areas where exposure would exceed the limits, or reduce power to reduce the field strengths in those areas. [97.13(c)(2), 1.1307(b)] [*General Class License Manual*, page 9-9]

G0A06 **What must you do if your station fails to meet the FCC RF exposure exemption criteria?**

A. Perform an RF Exposure Evaluation in accordance with FCC OET Bulletin 65
B. Contact the FCC for permission to transmit
C. Perform an RF exposure evaluation in accordance with World Meteorological Organization guidelines
D. Use an FCC-approved band-pass filter

(A) If you find that your station exceeds the exemption criteria listed in **Tables G0.1** and **G0.2**, you will need to evaluate it according to the FCC OET Bulletin 65. [97.13(c)(2), 1.1307(1)(b)(3)(i)] [*General Class License Manual*, page 9-9]

Table G0.1
Maximum Exempt ERP

Frequency (MHz)	Maximum ERP (Watts)
VLF	0.3 – 1.34	$1920 \times R^2$
HF	1.34 – 30	$3450 \times R^2 / f^2$
VHF	30 – 300	$3.83 \times R^2$
UHF	300 – 1500	$0.0128 \times R^2 \times f$
MW	1500 – 100,000	$19.2 \times R^2$

Note: R is distance in meters and f is frequency in MHz.
Example Calculations:

On 14.1 MHz at 10 meters from the antenna, the maximum exempt ERP is $3450 \times 10^2 / 14.1^2 = 1735$ W.

On 22.2 MHz at 10 meters from the antenna, the maximum exempt ERP is $3450 \times 10^2 / 22.2^2 = 433$ W.

On 50.1 MHz at 5 meters from the antenna, the maximum exempt ERP is $3.83 \times 5^2 = 96$ W.

On 146 MHz at 0.5 meters from the antenna, the maximum exempt ERP is $3.83 \times 0.5^2 = 0.96$ W.

Table G0.2
Minimum Exemption Distances ($\lambda/2\pi$)

Band (MHz)	Distance
1.8	87.0 ft
3.6	43.5 ft
3.9	40.2 ft
7.1	22.1 ft
10.1	15.5 ft
14.1	11.1 ft
18.1	8.7 ft
21.2	7.4 ft
24.9	6.3 ft
28.2	5.6 ft
50.1	3.1 ft
146	1.1 ft
223	8.4 in

G0A07 **What is the effect of modulation duty cycle on RF exposure?**

A. A lower duty cycle permits greater power levels to be transmitted
B. A higher duty cycle permits greater power levels to be transmitted
C. Low duty cycle transmitters are exempt from RF exposure evaluation requirements
D. High duty cycle transmitters are exempt from RF exposure requirements

(A) Since amateurs usually spend more time listening than transmitting, low duty cycles are common. Remember that including duty cycle in the exposure evaluation takes into account the reduced average transmitted power from not operating continuously at full power. This means greater short-term exposure levels can be permitted with low-duty-cycle emissions. [*General Class License Manual*, page 9-9]

G0A08 **Which of the following steps must an amateur operator take to ensure compliance with RF safety regulations?**

A. Post a copy of FCC Part 97.13 in the station
B. Notify neighbors within a 100-foot radius of the antenna of the existence of the station and power levels
C. Perform a routine RF exposure evaluation and prevent access to any identified high exposure areas
D. All these choices are correct

(C) Even if your station is exempt from the requirement, you may want to do a simple RF Radiation Exposure Evaluation. The results would demonstrate to yourself and possibly to your neighbors that your station is within the guidelines and is no cause for concern. None of the actions listed in the other answer choices would help to ensure that your station meets the FCC RF safety regulations. [97.13(c)(2)] [*General Class License Manual*, page 9-9]

G0A09 **What type of instrument can be used to accurately measure an RF field strength?**

A. A receiver with digital signal processing (DSP) noise reduction
B. A calibrated field strength meter with a calibrated antenna
C. An SWR meter with a peak-reading function
D. An oscilloscope with a high-stability crystal marker generator

(B) You can use a calibrated field-strength meter and calibrated field-strength sensor (antenna) to accurately measure an RF field. Even if you have access to such an expensive laboratory-grade field-strength meter, several factors can upset the readings. Reflections from the ground and nearby conductors (power lines, other antennas, house wiring, etc.) can easily confuse field-strength readings. You must know the frequency response of the test equipment and probes, and use them only within the appropriate range. Even the orientation of the test probe with respect to the polarization of the antenna being tested is important. [*General Class License Manual*, page 9-9]

G0A10 **What should be done if evaluation shows that a neighbor might experience more than the allowable limit of RF exposure from the main lobe of a directional antenna?**

A. Change to a non-polarized antenna with higher gain
B. Use an antenna with a higher front-to-back ratio
C. Take precautions to ensure that the antenna cannot be pointed in their direction when they are present
D. All these choices are correct

(C) A simple way to ensure that you do not point your antenna toward a neighbor's house while you are transmitting is to clearly mark your rotator control to remind you. Some rotator controls also have programmable "no go" regions that can prevent rotating the antenna to those directions. [*General Class License Manual*, page 9-9]

G0A11 **What precaution should you take if you install an indoor transmitting antenna?**

A. Locate the antenna close to your operating position to minimize feed-line radiation
B. Position the antenna along the edge of a wall to reduce parasitic radiation
C. Make sure that MPE limits are not exceeded in occupied areas
D. Make sure the antenna is properly shielded

(C) You should locate any antenna (whether it is indoors or outdoors) as far away as practical from living spaces that will be occupied while you are operating. You should also perform a routine environmental evaluation to make sure that MPE limits are not exceeded in occupied areas. [*General Class License Manual*, page 9-9]

G0A12 **What stations are subject to the FCC rules on RF exposure?**

A. All commercial stations; amateur radio stations are exempt
B. Only stations with antennas lower than one wavelength above the ground
C. Only stations transmitting more than 500 watts PEP
D. All stations with a time-averaged transmission of more than one milliwatt

(D) The rate at which energy is absorbed from the field to which the body is exposed is called the *specific absorption rate* (SAR). SAR is the best indicator of RF exposure but is unfortunately very difficult to determine. The SAR varies with frequency, power density, and the duty cycle of transmission. Injury can be caused when the combination of frequency and power result in excessive SAR that can lead to unacceptable tissue temperature rise.

SAR depends on the frequency and the size of the body or body part affected and is highest when the body and body parts are resonant. The limbs (arms and legs) and torso experience the highest SAR for RF fields in the VHF spectrum from 30 to 300 MHz. The head is more absorptive at UHF frequencies from 300 MHz to 3 GHz. The frequencies with highest whole-body SAR are between 30 and 1500 MHz. At frequencies above and below the ranges of highest absorption, the body as a whole responds less and less to the RF energy, just like an antenna responds poorly to signals away from its resonant frequency.

Safe exposure levels based on demonstrated hazards have been adopted by the FCC in the form of maximum permissible exposure (MPE) values (that may be used instead of whole-body SAR limits) that vary with frequency as shown in **Figure G0.1** and **Tables G0.3** and **G0.4**. These are much easier to measure or calculate and they take into account the variations in the body's absorption of RF energy at different frequencies. [1.1307(1)(b)(3)(i)(A)] [*General Class License Manual*, page 9-9]

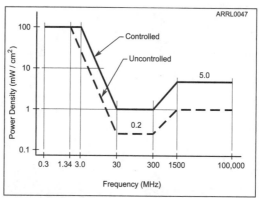

Figure G0.1 — Maximum Permissible Exposure (MPE) limits vary with frequency because the body responds differently to energy at different frequencies. The occupational (controlled) and general public (uncontrolled) limits refer to the characteristics of the people being exposed to the RF energy. The controlled limits apply to trained occupational exposure and amateurs. The uncontrolled limits apply to the general public.

Table G0.3
(From §1.1310) Limits for Maximum Permissible Exposure (MPE)
Limits for Occupational/Controlled Exposure

Frequency Range (MHz)	Electric Field Strength (V/m)	Magnetic Field Strength (A/m)	Power Density (mW/cm2)	Averaging Time (minutes)
0.3-3.0	614	1.63	(100)*	6
3.0-30	1842/f	4.89/f	(900/f2)*	6
30-300	61.4	0.163	1.0	6
300-1500	—	—	f/300	6
1500-100,000	—	—	5	6

f = frequency in MHz
* = Plane-wave equivalent power density (see Notes 1 and 2 in Table 9.3B).

Table G0.4
Limits for General Population/Uncontrolled Exposure

Frequency Range (MHz)	Electric Field Strength (V/m)	Magnetic Field Strength (A/m)	Power Density (mW/cm²)	Averaging Time (minutes)
0.3-1.34	614	1.63	(100)*	30
1.34-30	824/f	2.19/f	(180/f2)*	30
30-300	27.5	0.073	0.2	30
300-1500	—	—	f/1500	30
1500-100,000	—	—	1.0	30

f = frequency in MHz
* = Plane-wave equivalent power density (see Notes 1 and 2).

Note 1: This means the equivalent far-field strength that would have the E or H-field component calculated or measured. It does not apply well in the near field of an antenna. The equivalent far-field power density can be found in the near or far field regions from the relationships:

$Pd = |Etotal|2 / 3770$ mW/cm² or from $P_d = |H_{total}|^2 \times 37.7$ mW/cm².
Note 2: $|E_{total}|^2 = |E_x|^2 + |E_y|^2 + |E_z|^2$, and $|H_{total}|^2 = |H_x|^2 + |H_y|^2 + |H_z|^2$

G0B — Station safety: electrical shock, grounding, fusing, interlocks, and wiring; antenna and tower safety

G0B01 Which wire or wires in a four-conductor 240 VAC circuit should be attached to fuses or circuit breakers?

A. Only the hot wires
B. Only the neutral wire
C. Only the ground wire
D. All wires

(A) The hot wires (the wires carrying voltage) are the only ones that should be fused. If fuses are installed in the neutral or ground lines, an overload will open the fuses or circuit breaker but will *not* remove power from any equipment connected to that circuit. [*General Class License Manual*, page 9-4]

G0B02 According the National Electrical Code, what is the minimum wire size that may be used safely for wiring with a 20 ampere circuit breaker?

A. AWG number 20
B. AWG number 16
C. AWG number 12
D. AWG number 8

(C) AWG number 12 wire is required for a 20-ampere circuit. [*General Class License Manual*, page 9-4]

G0B03 Which size of fuse or circuit breaker would be appropriate to use with a circuit that uses AWG number 14 wiring?

A. 30 amperes
B. 25 amperes
C. 20 amperes
D. 15 amperes

(D) AWG number 14 wiring should be protected by a 15-ampere fuse or circuit breaker. [*General Class License Manual*, page 9-4]

Figure G0.2 — A metal entrance panel serves as a common grounding point for all cables and feed lines entering your home. The ground rod to which the panel is attached must also be connected to the ac service entry ground rod with a heavy bonding wire. This helps to prevent damage from lightning.

G0B04 Where should the station's lightning protection ground system be located?

A. As close to the station equipment as possible
B. Outside the building
C. Next to the closest power pole
D. Parallel to the water supply line

(B) The goal of lightning protection is to provide fire prevention for your home and to reduce or prevent electrical damage to your equipment. When installing your station, a metal entry panel where signal and control cables enter the house is a good place to provide a lightning ground (see **Figure G0.2**). The panel should be grounded to a nearby ground rod with a heavy, short metal strap. Lightning arrestors should be installed at the entry panel. The ground rod must then be bonded to the ac service entry ground rod outside the building with a heavy conductor. [*General Class License Manual*, page 9-8]

G0B05 Which of the following conditions will cause a ground fault circuit interrupter (GFCI) to disconnect AC power?

A. Current flowing from one or more of the hot wires to the neutral wire
B. Current flowing from one or more of the hot wires directly to ground
C. Overvoltage on the hot wires
D. All these choices are correct

(B) When you are performing electrical maintenance in your home or in the station, how can you tell what practices are safe? The *National Electrical Code Handbook* contains detailed descriptions of how to handle ac wiring in your home and station in a safe manner. (You may be able to get a copy at the library.)

Local building codes should also be followed so that your home is properly wired to meet any special local conditions. This may be important for insurance purposes, as well. If you are in doubt about your ability to do the work properly, hire a licensed professional electrician! [*General Class License Manual*, page 9-4]

G0B06 Which of the following is covered by the National Electrical Code?

A. Acceptable bandwidth limits
B. Acceptable modulation limits
C. Electrical safety of the station
D. RF exposure limits of the human body

(C) The National Electrical Code covers the wiring of electrical devices, [*General Class License Manual*, page 9-4]

G0B07 Which of these choices should be observed when climbing a tower using a safety harness?

A. Always hold on to the tower with one hand
B. Confirm that the harness is rated for the weight of the climber and that it is within its allowable service life
C. Ensure that all heavy tools are securely fastened to the harness
D. All these choices are correct

(B) As you are climbing up or down, remember to take your time — it's not a race! Be sure your climbing gear is fully secure:
• Belts and harnesses must be within their service life and adequately rated for weight
• Carabiners should be completely closed
• Latching hooks should close away from the tower
• Always use a safety lanyard or redundant lanyards
And remember that often forgotten rule: follow the manufacturer's directions!
[*General Class License Manual*, page 9-14]

G0B08 What should be done before climbing a tower that supports electrically powered devices?

A. Notify the electric company that a person will be working on the tower
B. Make sure all circuits that supply power to the tower are locked out and tagged
C. Unground the base of the tower
D. All these choices are correct

(B) Before climbing, remove power from any circuit that will not be used while you are on the tower. The best way is to remove fuses or open circuit breakers. Once the circuit is opened, lock the circuit breaker open, if possible, and tag the fuse block or breaker panel so that no one will reconnect the circuit. [*General Class License Manual*, page 9-14]

G0B09 **Which of the following is true of an emergency generator installation?**

A. The generator should be operated in a well-ventilated area
B. The generator must be insulated from ground
C. Fuel should be stored near the generator for rapid refueling in case of an emergency
D. All these choices are correct

(A)   Fueling and ventilation problems cause more injuries associated with generators than from any other cause. A generator should never be operated in an enclosed space or basement, or even a garage, where people are present or nearby. Install it outdoors, away from living areas. Carbon monoxide (CO) in the exhaust can quickly build up to toxic levels. (For more information about CO safety, visit **epa.gov/indoor-air-quality-iaq/carbon-monoxides-impact-indoor-air-quality**.) Even outside, exhaust fumes can be drawn into air intakes or windows or build up in poorly ventilated areas. If you plan on using a generator regularly, install CO detector alarms in living and working areas. [*General Class License Manual*, page 9-7]

G0B10   **Which of the following is a danger from lead-tin solder?**

A. Lead can contaminate food if hands are not washed carefully after handling the solder
B. High voltages can cause lead-tin solder to disintegrate suddenly
C. Tin in the solder can "cold flow," causing shorts in the circuit
D. RF energy can convert the lead into a poisonous gas

(A)   Lead is a known toxin when ingested or inhaled. Although the amount of soldering done by most amateurs does not cause enough lead exposure to be a hazard, it is a good idea to wash your hands after soldering and not eat "at the bench." [*General Class License Manual*, page 9-6]

G0B11   **Which of the following is required for lightning protection ground rods?**

A. They must be bonded to all buried water and gas lines
B. Bends in ground wires must be made as close as possible to a right angle
C. Lightning grounds must be connected to all ungrounded wiring
D. They must be bonded together with all other grounds

(D)   Lightning protection grounds must be tied to all other safety grounds in your home and shack. Having separate ground systems can expose equipment to damage from the lightning current jumping between ground systems. [*General Class License Manual*, page 9-8]

G0B12 What is the purpose of a power supply interlock?

A. To prevent unauthorized changes to the circuit that would void the manufacturer's warranty
B. To shut down the unit if it becomes too hot
C. To ensure that dangerous voltages are removed if the cabinet is opened
D. To shut off the power supply if too much voltage is produced

(C) High voltages are often present inside transmitter and amplifier power supplies. The interlocks on those supplies prevent you from coming in contact with energized power supply components. Interlocks often short high voltage circuits to ground when activated, providing further safety measures. Do not defeat or bypass interlock circuits unless the repair instructions specifically require you to do so. [*General Class License Manual*, page 9-4]

G0B13 Where should lightning arrestors be located?

A. Where the feed lines enter the building
B. On the antenna, opposite the feed point
C. In series with each ground lead
D. At the closest power pole ground electrode

(A) See G0B04. [*General Class License Manual*, page 9-8]

PreppComm
Amateur Radio   www.preppcomm.com

Real preppers use PreppComm™

Emergency Comm That Works™

MOSLEY ANTENNAS

Mosley

AIRCRAFT GRADE ALUMINUM
ELEMENTS & BOOMS and
STAINLESS STEEL HARDWARE

..."a better Antenna!"

STRONG!
Snow, ice or rain
are no match for
Mosley Quality!

...built to last!

Call 800-325-4016
REQUEST A CATALOG
www.mosley-electronics.com
or
www.mosleyelectronics.com

The ARRL General Class License Manual

Index of Advertisers

Air Boss Antenna Launcher

$99.99

See Video
www.olahtechnologies.com

When you want your
antenna on top

Free shipping
to
lower 48

Every AirBoss
Earns It's Sticker

My Grandfather (KR4LO)
instilled in me that you have an
obligation to every customer to
provide a good quality working
product to every buyer. You can
buy with confidence knowing
that every AirBoss undergoes
quality control prior to leaving
my shop. All AirBosses are
pressure tested and sinker
tested prior to receiving its
sticker and being packaged.

olahtechnologies@gmail.com

Upgrade to
Amateur Extra with
The ARRL Extra Class
License Manual

EXTRA CLASS
LICENSE MANUAL

www.arrl.org/shop

Remove noise and listen clearly with..
..a bhi DSP noise canceling product! **bhi**

ParaPro EQ20
Audio DSP Range

- improved audio for those with hearing loss
- Two separate mono inputs or one stereo input
- Use with passive speakers or headphones
- Basic EQ units EQ20, EQ20B (use with Dual In-Line, Compact In-Line or In-Line Module)
- DSP noise canceling versions EQ20-DSP, EQ20B-DSP with added Bluetooth on input
QST Dec 2019 review "easy-to-use device that improves the audio clarity of amateur signals"

In-Line Module

Dual In-Line

- 5W amplified DSP noise canceling In-Line module
- 8 filter levels 8 to 40dB
- Use in-line with a loudspeaker
Great review in Jan '23 QST!

Fully featured dual channel DSP noise canceling unit
- 8 Filter levels 9 to 40dB
- 3.5mm speaker level & line level inputs
- separate 7W mono speaker output- Headphone socket
- Easy to use controls

NES10-2MK4   **DESKTOP MKII**

Compact In-Line

5W amplified DSP noise canceling speaker
- Compact speaker for mobile or base station
- Audio bypass feature

- Portable DSP noise canceling unit
- Simple controls
- Use in-line with speakers or headphones
- Line/speaker level inputs - Use with AA batteries or 12V DC

New NEDSP1962-KBD 5W amplified DSP noise canceling speaker retrofit pcb module now available!

10W amplified DSP noise canceling speaker
- Simple controls
- 8 filter levels
- Separate line level and speaker level audio inputs
- 12V DC power

DX ENGINEERING
DXEngineering.com -1-800-777-0703

GigaParts 256-428-4644
www.bhi-ltd.com

VISA PayPal MasterCard

TAP INTO OUR GENIUS SOLUTIONS AND MAKE EVERYTHING AROUND YOU FEEL SMARTER.

Genius products are engineered to work so well in tandem, expanding your station's ability to deliver exceptional experiences and exponential performance increases. Add a Power Genius XL and get the only legal-limit SO2R/Multi-Singlecapable HF/6M amplifier on the market. Add a Tuner Genious XL and gain not only super-fast, legal-limit impedance matching on antennas with up to 10:1 SWR but then pick up 70dB of port isolation for seamless SO2R operation. Add an Antenna Genius and enjoy frequency-driven contest-class SO2R antenna switching and super-station automation capabilities. With integration this easy, our Genius Solutions help you realize the potential of your station, making you genius-level smart along the way. Learn more at **FlexRadio.com**

FlexRadio

Find Everywhere

IT'S TOTALLY NORMAL TO SUDDENLY FEEL LIKE THE SMARTEST PERSON ON THE PLANET.

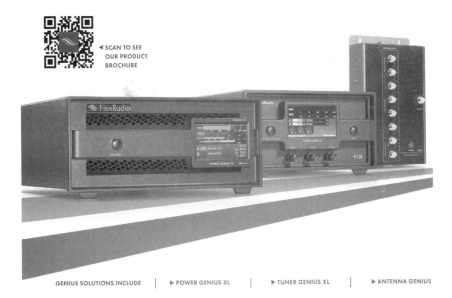

◀ SCAN TO SEE OUR PRODUCT BROCHURE

GENIUS SOLUTIONS INCLUDE | ▶ POWER GENIUS XL | ▶ TUNER GENIUS XL | ▶ ANTENNA GENIUS

HAM RADIO OUTLET

WWW.HAMRADIO.COM

Free Shipping and Fast Delivery!

IC-9700 | *All Mode Tri-Band Transceiver*
• VHF/UHF/1.2GHz • Direct Sampling Now Enters the VHF/UHF Arena • 4.3" Touch Screen Color TFT LCD • Real-Time, High-Speed Spectrum Scope & Waterfall Display • Smooth Satellite Operation

IC-7851 | *HF/50MHz Transceiver*
• 1.2kHz "Optimum" roofing filter • New local oscillator design • Improved phase noise • Improved spectrum scope • Dual scope function • Enhanced mouse operation for spectrum scope

IC-7300 | *HF/50MHz Transceiver*
• RF Direct Sampling System • New "IP+" Function • Class Leading RMDR and Phase Noise Characteristics • 15 Discrete Band-Pass Filters • Built-In Automatic Antenna Tuner

IC-7610 | *HF/50 MHz All Mode Transceiver*
• Large 7-inch color display with high resolution real-time spectrum scope and waterfall • Independent direct sampling receivers capable of receiving two bands/two modes simultaneously

IC-R8600 | *Wideband SDR Receiver*
10 kHz to 3 GHz Super Wideband Coverage • Real-time Spectrum Scope w/Waterfall Function • Remote Control Function through IP Network or USB Cable • Decodes Digital incl P25, NXDN™, D-STAR • SD Card Slot for Receiver Recorder

IC-718 | *HF Transceiver*
• 160-10M** • 100W • 12V operation • Simple to use • CW Keyer Built-in • One touch band switching • Direct frequency input • VOX Built-in • Band stacking register • IF shift • 101 memories

IC-705 | *HF/50/144/430 MHz All Mode Transceiver*
• RF Direct Sampling • Real-Time Spectrum Scope and Waterfall Display • Large Color Touch Screen • Supports QRP/QRPp • Bluetooth® and Wireless LAN Built-in

IC-7100 | *All Mode Transceiver*
• HF/50/144/430/440 MHz Multi-band, Multi-mode, IF DSP • D-STAR DV Mode (Digital Voice + Data) • Intuitive Touch Screen Interface • Built-in RTTY Functions

IC-2730A | *VHF/VHF Dual Band Transceiver*
• VHF/VHF, UHF/UHF simultaneous receive • 50 watts of output on VHF and UHF • Optional VS-3 Bluetooth® headset • Easy-to-See large white backlight LCD • Controller attachment to the main Unit

ID-5100A Deluxe
VHF/UHF Dual Band Digital Transceiver
• Analog FM/D-Star DV Mode • SD Card Slot for Voice & Data Storage • 50W Output on VHF/UHF Bands • Integrated GPS Receiver • AM Airband Dualwatch

IC-V3500 | *144MHz FM Mobile*
• 65W of Power for Long Range Communications • 4.5 Watts Loud & Clear Audio • Modern White Display & Simple Operation • Weather Channel Receive & Alert Function

IC-2300H | *VHF FM Transceiver*
• 65W RF Output Power • 4.5W Audio Output • MIL-STD 810 G Specifications • 207 alphanumeric Memory Channels • Built-in CTCSS/DTCS Encode/Decode • DMS

IC-V86 | *VHF 7W HT*
• 7W Output Power Plus New Antenna Provides 1.5 Times More Coverage • More Audio, 1500 mW Audio Output • IP54 & MIL-STD 810G–Rugged Design Against Dust & Water • 19 Hours of Long Lasting Battery Life • 200 Memory Channels, 1 Call Channel & 6 Scan Edges

IC-T10 | *Rugged 144/430 MHz Dual Band*
• Disaster Ready - Excellent Fit for Your Emergency Bag • Loud Audio - New Speaker Design • Long Battery Life - Up to 11 Hours • FM Broadcast & Weather Channels

ID-52A | *VHF/UHF D-STAR Portable*
• Bluetooth® Communication • Simultaneous Reception in V/V, U/U, V/U and DV/DV • Enriched D-STAR® Features Including the Terminal Mode/Access Point Mode • UHF (225–374.995MHz) Air Band Reception

5 Ways to Shop!
• RETAIL LOCATIONS – Store hours 10:00AM - 5:30PM - Closed Sunday
• PHONE – Toll-free phone hours 9:30AM - 5:30PM
• ONLINE – WWW.HAMRADIO.COM
• FAX – All store locations
• MAIL – All store locations

ICOM

FOLLOW HRO ON SOCIAL MEDIA
twitter.com/HamRadioOutlet
facebook.com/HROHamRadioOutlet
instagram.com/HamRadioOutlet
youtube.com/HamRadioOutlet

*On most orders over $100 in the continental US. (Rural locations excluded.) **Except 60M Band. The Icom logo is a registered trademark of Icom Inc. Toll-free including Hawaii, Alaska and Canada. All HRO 800-lines can assist you if the first line you call is busy, you may call another. Prices, specifications and descriptions subject to change without notice.

HAM RADIO OUTLET®

WWW.HAMRADIO.COM

Family owned and operated since 1971

FTDX101MP | *200W HF/50MHz Transceiver*
• Hybrid SDR Configuration • Unparalleled 70 dB Max. Attenuation VC-Tune • New Generation Scope Display 3DSS • ABI (Active Band Indicator) & MPVD (Multi-Purpose VFO Outer Dial) • PC Remote Control Software to Expand the Operating Range • Includes External Power With Matching Front Speaker

FTDX10 | *HF/50MHz 100 W SDR Transceiver*
• Narrow Band and Direct Sampling SDR • Down Conversion, 9MHz IF Roofing Filters Produce Excellent Shape Factor • 5" Full-Color Touch Panel w/3D Spectrum Stream • High Speed Auto Antenna Tuner • Microphone Amplifier w/3-Stage Parametric Equalizer • Remote Operation w/optional LAN Unit (SCU-LAN10)

FT-991A | *HF/VHF/UHF All ModeTransceiver*
Real-time Spectrum Scope with Automatic Scope Control • Multi-color waterfall display • State of the art 32-bit Digital Signal Processing System • 3kHz Roofing Filter for enhanced performance • 3.5 Inch Full Color TFT USB Capable • Internal Automatic Antenna Tuner • High Accuracy TCXO

FTDX101D | *HF + 6M Transceiver*
• Narrow Band SDR & Direct Sampling SDR • Crystal Roofing Filters Phenomenal Multi-Signal Receiving Characteristics • Unparalleled - 70dB Maximum Attenuation VC-Tune • 15 Separate (HAM 10 + GEN 5) Powerful Band Pass Filters • New Generation Scope Displays 3-Dimensional Spectrum Stream

FT-710 Aess | *HF/50MHz 100W SDR Transceiver*
• Unmatched SDR Receiving Performance • Band Pass Filters Dedicated for the Amateur Bands • High Res 4.3-inch TFT Color Touch Display • AESS: Acoustic Enhanced Speaker System with SP-40 For High-Fidelity Audio • Built-in High Speed Auto Antenna Tuner

FT-891 | *HF+50 MHz All Mode Mobile Transceiver*
Stable 100 Watt Output • 32-Bit IF DSP • Large Dot Matrix LCD Display with Quick Spectrum Scope • USB Port Allows Connection to a PC with a Single Cable • CAT Control, PTT/RTTY Control

FTM-300DR | *C4FM/FM 144/430MHz Dual Band*
• 50W Output Power • Real Dual Band Operation • Full Color TFT Display • Band Scope • Built-in Bluetooth • WIRES-X Portable Digital Node/Fixed Node with HRI-200

FTM-500DR | *2M/440 Mobile*
• FM, APRS and Digital Voice (C4FM) Operation • Built-in GPS Receiver with 66 Channels • Large Easy-to-Read LCD Display • Front speaker with AESS

FTM-200DR | *C4FM/FM 144/430MHz Dual Band*
• 1200/9600bps APRS® Data Communications • 2" High-Res Full-Color TFT Display • High-Speed Band Scope • Advanced C4FM Digital Mode • Voice Recording Function for TX/RX

FTM-3100R | *Rugged 65W 2M FM Transceiver*
• Rugged & Compact • Crystal Clear Front Panel Audio • 220 Memory Channels • Weather Broadcast Reception • Severe Weather Alert Feature

FT-70DR *C4FM/FM 144/430MHz Xcvr*
• System Fusion Compatible • Large Front Speaker delivers 700 mW of Loud Audio Output • Automatic Mode Select detects C4FM or Fm Analog and Switches Accordingly • Huge 1,105 Channel Memory Capacity • External DC Jack for DC Supply and Battery Charging

FT-5DR *C4FM/FM 144/430 MHz Dual Band*
• High-Res Full-Color Touch Screen TFT LCD Display • Easy Hands-Free Operation w/Built-In Bluetooth® Unit • Built-In High Precision GPS Antenna • 1200/9600bps APRS Data Communications • Supports Simultaneous C4FM Digital • Micro SD Card Slot

FT-65R | *144/430 MHz Transceiver*
Compact Commercial Grade Rugged Design • Large Front Speaker Delivers 1W of Powerful Clear Audio • 5 Watts of Reliable RF Power With-in a compact Body • 3.5-Hour Rapid Charger Included • Large White LED Flashlight, Alarm and Quick Home Channel Access

FTM-6000R | *50W VHF/UHF Mobile Transceiver*
• All New User Operating Interface-E20-III (Easy to Operate-III) • Robust Speaker Delivers 3W of Clear, Crisp Receive Audio • Detachable Front Panel Can Be Mounted in Multiple Positions • Supports Optional Bluetooth® Wireless Operation Using the SSM-BT10 or a Commercially Available Bluetooth® Headset

5 Ways to Shop!

• RETAIL LOCATIONS – Store hours 10:00AM – 5:30PM – Closed Sunday
• PHONE – Toll-free phone hours 9:30AM – 5:30PM   • FAX – All store locations
• ONLINE – WWW.HAMRADIO.COM   • MAIL – All store locations

YAESU
The radio

ANAHEIM, CA	PORTLAND, OR	PHOENIX, AZ	MILWAUKEE, WI	WOODBRIDGE, VA	WINTER SPRINGS, FL
(800) 854-6046	(800) 765-4267	(800) 559-7388	(800) 558-0411	(800) 444-4799	(800) 327-1917
SACRAMENTO, CA	DENVER, CO	PLANO, TX	NEW CASTLE, DE	SALEM, NH	ATLANTA, GA
(877) 892-1745	(800) 444-9476	(877) 455-8750	(800) 644-4476	(800) 444-0047	(800) 444-7927

Contact HRO for promotion details. Toll-free including Hawaii, Alaska and Canada. All HRO 800-lines can assist you. If the first line you call is busy, you may call another. Prices, specifications and descriptions subject to change without notice.

SOTA, POTA, or Shack
Icom has the HF lineup you want

IC-705
HF / 6M / 2M / 70CM Transceiver

IC-7300
HF / 6M SDR Transceiver

IC-7610
HF / 6M SDR Transceiver

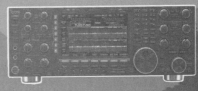

IC-7851
HF / 6M Transceiver

For the love of **ham radio.**

www.icomamerica.com/amateur
insidesales@icomamerica.com

ICOM

Made In
the U.S.A.

CABLE X-PERTS INC. IS A MANUFACTURER OF HIGH-QUALITY CABLE ASSEMBLIES.

We are proud to be a part of Seminole Wire & Cable family of brands which includes JSC brand coaxial cables. We achieve fastest in the industry order delivery by consolidating stock of cables and assembly materials. All raw materials are carefully sourced, and cable is manufactured in Pennsauken, NJ.

OUR PL-259 CONNECTOR IS SPECIFICALLY DESIGNED AND MADE FOR CABLE X-PERTS

RG-8X COAXIAL ASSEMBLY-15YR GUARANTEE

ATTENUATION		KEY FEATURES
MHz	db/100ft	HF applications 1-30 MHz
1	0.3	Maximum 875 Watts
10	0.9	Lightweight and portable
30	2	Direct Burial with waterproof shrink tubing
50	2.3	Standard lengths (ft): 1.5, 3, 6, 9, 12, 18, 25, 50, 75, 100, 150.

RG-213 COAXIAL ASSEMBLY-15YR GUARANTEE

ATTENUATION		KEY FEATURES
MHz	db/100ft	MIL-C-17
10	0.55	Non-Migrating PVC Jacket
50	1.3	LOW LOSS HF COAX
100	1.9	Direct Burial with waterproof shrink tubing
200	2.7	Standard lengths (ft): 1.5, 3, 6, 9, 12, 18, 25, 50, 75, 100, 150.

RG-8/U COAXIAL ASSEMBLY-15YR GUARANTEE

ATTENUATION		KEY FEATURES
MHz	db/100ft	LOW LOSS
10	0.47	Durable UV Resistant, PVC Jacket
50	1.2	1 – 50 MHz or 6 METERS
100	1.8	Direct Burial with waterproof shrink tubing
200	2.7	Standard lengths (ft): 1.5, 3, 6, 9, 12, 18, 25, 50, 75, 100, 150.

CABLE X-PERTS, INC.
Connecting You to the World...

400UF COAXIAL ASSEMBLY-15YR GUARANTEE (9913 Type)

ATTENUATION		KEY FEATURES
MHz	db/100ft	LMR-400-UF (BELDEN 9913) TYPE
30	0.8	Non-Migrating PVC Jacket
50	1.1	LOW LOSS UHF/VHF
150	1.8	Direct Burial with waterproof shrink tubing
450	3.3	Standard lengths (ft): 1.5, 3, 6, 9, 12, 18, 25, 50, 75, 100, 150.

DBFLEX400 COAXIAL ASSEMBLY-20YR GUARANTEE

ATTENUATION		KEY FEATURES
MHz	db/100ft	FLEXIBLE LOW LOSS 400
30	0.8	UV and Weather Resistant PE Jacket
50	1.1	LOW LOSS UHF/VHF
150	1.8	Direct Burial with waterproof shrink tubing
450	3.3	Standard lengths (ft): 1.5, 3, 6, 9, 12, 18, 25, 50, 75, 100, 150.

LMR400 TYPE COAXIAL ASSEMBLY-20YR GUARANTEE

ATTENUATION		KEY FEATURES
MHz	db/100ft	LMR-400 TYPE, SOLID CONDUCTOR
30	0.7	UV and Weather Resistant PE Jacket
50	0.9	LOW LOSS UHF/VHF
150	1.5	Direct Burial with waterproof shrink tubing
450	2.7	Standard lengths (ft): 1.5, 3, 6, 9, 12, 18, 25, 50, 75, 100, 150.

SALES AND CUSTOM ASSEMBLIES
1(800)828-3340
WWW.CABLEXPERTS.COM
Look for 'Cable Experts' on Amazon

EVERYWHERE MEANS EVERYWHERE.

As the pioneers of software-defined radios, we didn't set out to change the course of the entire amateur radio industry, but it kind of turned out that way. When you're looking to connect with people and places that may or may not even be on the map, you better have the best technology partner on the planet. We revolutionize for the love of amateur radio and the community that goes along with it. We aim higher and look farther in hopes of creating tools and solutions for things we can't even see just yet. We are your best partner to Find Everywhere. **FlexRadio.com**

FlexRadio

Find Everywhere

THROW A DART AT A MAP. THEN HAVE A MEANINGFUL CONVERSATION WITH THE DART.

SCAN TO SEE ▶
OUR PRODUCT
BROCHURE

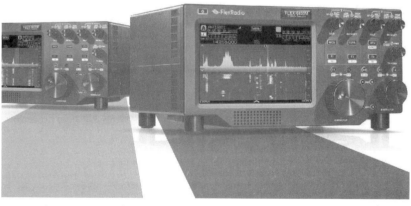

6400 | 6400M | 6600 | 6600M | 6700 | MAESTRO A-9

www.W5SWL.com

Premium Quality RF Connectors Order Direct !

Wide Selection of Connectors

- *UHF & N*
- *BNC & SMA*
- *Mini-UHF & FME*
- *TNC & C*
- *MC MCX & MMCX*

- *QMA SMB & SMC*
- *DIN & Low PIM*
- *Reverse Polarity*
- *RF Adapters*
- *Bulkheads*

And Much More!

- *Dave's Hobby Shop by W5SWL*
- *Ham Radio Gadgets*
- *RF Technical Parts*
- *New & Surplus Materials*

- *Order at www.W5SWL.com*

Ships Fast From The Arkansas River Valley

Notes

Notes